Disposable Youth, Racialized Memories, and the Culture of Cruelty

Henry A. Giroux

Facing a crisis unlike that of any other generation, young people are caught between the discourses of consumerism and a powerful crime-control complex, and are viewed increasingly as commodities or are subjected to the dictates of an ever expanding criminal justice system. Drawing upon critical analyses, autobiography, and social theory, *Disposable Youth, Racialized Memories, and the Culture of Cruelty* explores the current conditions young people now face within an emerging culture of privatization, insecurity, and commodification, and raises some important questions regarding the role that educators, young people, and concerned citizens might play in challenging the plight of youth while deepening and extending the promise of a better future and a viable democracy.

Henry A. Giroux currently holds the Global TV Network Chair Professorship at McMaster University in the English and Cultural Studies Department. His most recent books include: *Youth in a Suspect Society: Democracy or Disposability?* (2009); *Zombie Politics and Culture in the Age of Casino Capitalism* (2011); *On Critical Pedagogy* (2011); and *Education and the Crisis of Public Values* (2012). His website can be found at www.henryagiroux.com.

Framing 21st Century Social Issues

The goal of this new, unique Series is to offer readable, teachable "thinking frames" on today's social problems and social issues by leading scholars. These are available for view on http://routledge.customgateway.com/routledge-social-issues.html.

For instructors teaching a wide range of courses in the social sciences, the Routledge *Social Issues Collection* now offers the best of both worlds: originally written short texts that provide "overviews" to important social issues *as well as* teachable excerpts from larger works previously published by Routledge and other presses.

As an instructor, click to the website to view the library and decide how to build your custom anthology and which thinking frames to assign. Students can choose to receive the assigned materials in print and/or electronic formats at an affordable price.

Available

Body Problems
Running and Living Long in a Fast-Food Society
Ben Agger

Sex, Drugs, and Death
Addressing Youth Problems in American Society
Tammy Anderson

The Stupidity Epidemic
Worrying About Students, Schools, and America's Future
Joel Best

Empire Versus Democracy
The Triumph of Corporate and Military Power
Carl Boggs

Contentious Identities
Ethnic, Religious, and Nationalist Conflicts in Today's World
Daniel Chirot

The Future of Higher Education
Dan Clawson and Max Page

Waste and Consumption
Capitalism, the Environment, and the Life of Things
Simonetta Falasca-Zamponi

Rapid Climate Change
Causes, Consequences, and Solutions
Scott G. McNall

The Problem of Emotions in Societies
Jonathan H. Turner

Outsourcing the Womb
Race, Class, and Gestational Surrogacy in a Global Market
France Winddance Twine

Changing Times for Black Professionals
Adia Harvey Wingfield

Disposable Youth, Racialized Memories, and the Culture of Cruelty

Henry A. Giroux

McMaster University

Routledge
Taylor & Francis Group

NEW YORK AND LONDON

First published 2012
by Routledge
711 Third Avenue, New York, NY 10017

Simultaneously published in the UK
by Routledge
2 Park Square, Milton Park, Abingdon, Oxon OX14 4RN

Routledge is an imprint of the Taylor & Francis Group, an informa business

Library of Congress Cataloging in Publication Data
Giroux, Henry A.
    Disposable youth, racialized memories, and the culture of cruelty / Henry A. Giroux.
    p. cm. — (Framing 21st century social issues)
    1. Youth—United States—Social conditions—21st century. 2. Youth with social disabilities—United States. I. Title.
    HQ796.G5255 2011
    305.2350973—dc23
    2011039701

ISBN13: 978-0-415-50813-1 (pbk)
ISBN13: 978-0-203-12593-9 (ebk)

Typeset in Garamond and Gill Sans
by EvS Communication Networx, Inc.

University Readers (www.universityreaders.com): Since 1992, University Readers has been a leading custom publishing service, providing reasonably priced, copyright-cleared, course packs, custom textbooks, and custom publishing services in print and digital formats to thousands of professors nationwide. The Routledge Custom Gateway provides easy access to thousands of readings from hundreds of books and articles via an online library. The partnership of University Readers and Routledge brings custom publishing expertise and deep academic content together to help professors create perfect course materials that are affordable for students.

For Tolu
To young people the world over in their fight for a
more just and democratic future

Contents

Series Foreword

The world in the early 21st century is beset with problems—a troubled economy, global warming, oil spills, religious and national conflict, poverty, HIV, health problems associated with sedentary lifestyles. Virtually no nation is exempt, and everyone, even in affluent countries, feels the impact of these global issues.

Since its inception in the 19th century, sociology has been the academic discipline dedicated to analyzing social problems. It is still so today. Sociologists offer not only diagnoses; they glimpse solutions, which they then offer to policy makers and citizens who work for a better world. Sociology played a major role in the civil rights movement during the 1960s in helping us to understand racial inequalities and prejudice, and it can play a major role today as we grapple with old and new issues.

This series builds on the giants of sociology, such as Weber, Durkheim, Marx, Parsons, Mills. It uses their frames, and newer ones, to focus on particular issues of contemporary concern. These books are about the nuts and bolts of social problems, but they are equally about the frames through which we analyze these problems. It is clear by now that there is no single correct way to view the world, but only paradigms, models, which function as lenses through which we peer. For example, in analyzing oil spills and environmental pollution, we can use a frame that views such outcomes as unfortunate results of a reasonable effort to harvest fossil fuels. "Drill, baby, drill" sometimes involves certain costs as pipelines rupture and oil spews forth. Or we could analyze these environmental crises as inevitable outcomes of our effort to dominate nature in the interest of profit. The first frame would solve oil spills with better environmental protection measures and clean-ups, while the second frame would attempt to prevent them altogether, perhaps shifting away from the use of petroleum and natural gas and toward alternative energies that are "green."

These books introduce various frames such as these for viewing social problems. They also highlight debates between social scientists who frame problems differently. The books suggest solutions, on both the macro and micro levels. That is, they suggest what new policies might entail, and they also identify ways in which people, from the ground level, can work toward a better world, changing themselves and their lives and families and providing models of change for others.

Readers do not need an extensive background in academic sociology to benefit from these books. Each book is student-friendly in that we provide glossaries of terms for the uninitiated that are keyed to bolded terms in the text. The level of each book is accessible to undergraduate students, even as these books offer sophisticated and innovative analyses.

Henry A. Giroux's book confronts a crisis unlike that of any other generation, as young people are caught between the discourses of consumerism and a powerful crime-control complex, and are viewed increasingly as commodities or are subject to the dictates of an ever-expanding criminal justice system.

Drawing upon critical analyses, autobiography, and social theory, Giroux's *Disposable Youth, Racialized Memories, and the Culture of Cruelty* explores the current conditions young people face within an emerging culture of privatization and insecurity, and raises important questions regarding the roles that educators, young people, and concerned citizens might play in challenging the plight of young people while deepening and extending the promise of a better future and a viable democracy. He not only critiques; he glimpses solutions.

Preface

Youth Matters: Democracy Under Siege

Children are the future of any society. If you want to know the future of a society look at the eyes of the children. If you want to maim the future of any society, you simply maim the children. Thus the struggle for the survival of our children is the struggle for the survival of our future. The quantity and quality of that survival is the measurement of the development of our society.

Ngugi Wa Thiong'o (1993: 76)

Youth and the Crisis of the Future

A central theme of this book is that any discourse about the future has to begin with the issue of youth because young people embody the projected dreams, desires, and commitment of a society's obligations to the future. In many respects, youth not only register symbolically the importance of America's claim to progress; they also affirm the importance of the liberal democratic tradition of the social contract in which adult responsibility is mediated through a willingness to fight for the rights of children, enact reforms that invest in their future, and provide the educational conditions necessary for them to make use of the freedoms they have, while learning how to be **critical citizens**. Within such a modernist project, democracy is linked to the well-being of youth, while the status of how a society imagines democracy and its future is contingent on how it views its responsibility towards future generations. But the category of youth does more than affirm democracy's social contract, rooted in a conception of the future in which adult commitment and intergenerational solidarity are articulated as a vital public service. It also affirms those representations, images, vocabularies, values, and social relations central to a politics capable of both defending vital institutions as a public good and contributing to the quality of public life.

Yet as the 21st century unfolds, it is not at all clear that the American public and government believe any longer in youth, the future, or the social contract, even in its minimalist version. Since the 1980s, the prevailing market-inspired discourse dictates that there is no such thing as society and, indeed, following that nefarious pronouncement, institutions committed to public welfare, especially for young people, have been disappearing ever since. Those of us who, against the prevailing common sense, believe that the ultimate test of morality resides in what a society does for its children cannot help but acknowledge that if we take this standard seriously, American society has deeply failed its children and its commitment to democracy.

Lauded as a symbol of hope for the future while scorned as a threat to the existing social order, youth have become objects of ambivalence caught between contradictory representations, discourses, and spaces of transition. While pushed to the margins of political power within society, youth nonetheless become a central focus of adult fascination, desire, and authority, especially in the realm of popular culture. Increasingly denied opportunities for self-definition and political interaction, youth are transfigured by representations, discourses, and practices that subordinate and contain the language of individual freedom, social power, and critical agency. Symbols of a declining democracy, youth are located within a range of signifiers that largely deny their representational status as active citizens.

At stake here is not merely how American culture is redefining the meaning of youth, but how it constructs children in relation to a future devoid of the moral and political obligations of citizenship, social responsibility, and democracy. Caught up in an age of increasing despair, youth no longer appear to inspire adults to reaffirm their commitment to a public discourse that envisions a future in which human suffering is diminished while the general welfare of society is increased. On the contrary, youth today are reduced to an invisible category in the right-wing drive to hollow out social protections, defund public schools and colleges, dismantle job-creating programs for young people, and eliminate important social protections, especially for youth marginalized by class and color. Constructed primarily within the language of the market and the increasingly conservative politics of media culture, contemporary youth appear unable to constitute themselves through a defining generational referent that gives them a sense of distinctiveness and vision, as did the generation of youth in the 1960s. Not only do hyper-market-driven societies organize their identities largely as consumers, they offer few spaces where they can recognize themselves outside of the values, needs, and desires preferred by the market. The relations between youth and adults have always been marked by strained generational and ideological struggles, but the new economic and social conditions that youth face today, along with a callous indifference to their spiritual and material needs, suggest a qualitatively different attitude on the part of many adults toward American youth—one that indicates that the young have become our lowest national priority. When adult society talks about children, if they are mentioned at all, they are usually described as commodities or threats to our society. Young people have become dangerous in the current moment because they remind the American public that, for the last 30 years or so, their future has been shamelessly mortgaged by the savage politics and economics of casino capitalism. For instance, the primary social agencies that bear down on the lives of young people—

education, medicine, and the law—are increasingly constructed against the best interests of most young people. The disinvestment in education means that children often have to either pay for their own education or receive an education that amounts to nothing more than an instrumentalized form of training. And just as society disinvests in schools as democratic public spheres, they have opened the floodgates for corporations to commercialize education, promoting everything from junk food and field trips to corporate-owned chain stores and advertising in school hallways and gyms. Moreover, large numbers of youth are routinely denied health care while the medical profession subjects them more and more to psychopharmacological treatments for almost any behavior that is labeled as transgressive. Most importantly, the law has been refashioned less to protect young people than to treat the most minor behavior infractions in schools as criminal acts, resulting in an upsurge of children who are suspended, arrested, and jailed. Put bluntly, American society at present exudes both a deep-rooted hostility and chilling fear about youth, reinforcing the dismal conditions that young people are increasingly living under.

As I state throughout this book, punishment and fear have replaced compassion and social responsibility as the most important modalities mediating the relationship of youth to the larger social order. Youth within the last four decades are increasingly represented in the media as a source of trouble rather than as a resource for investing in the future and are increasingly either treated as a disposable population and cannon fodder for barbaric wars abroad, or defined as the source of most of society's problems. Youth, particularly young people marginalized by class and color, appear to live in a state of perpetual and unending emergency. Young people now constitute a crisis that has less to do with improving the future than with denying it. This was exemplified in an article by *New York Times* columnist Bob Herbert, who reported that "parts of New York City are like a police state for young men, women and children who happen to be black or Hispanic. They are routinely stopped, searched, harassed, intimidated, humiliated and, in many cases, arrested for no good reason" (Herbert 2007: A25). No longer "viewed as a privileged sign and embodiment of the future" (Grossberg 2001: 133), youth are now increasingly demonized by the popular media and derided by politicians looking for quick-fix solutions to crime and other social ills. In short, many young people, especially those who are poor and underprivileged, are considered excess, if not disposable, especially to a government that denies the importance of social protections and long-term investments, and is unconcerned about the social costs of what might be called the reign of **casino capitalism**.

Under the rule of neoliberal politics with its hyped-up social Darwinism and theater of cruelty, the popular demonization of the young now justifies responses to youth that were unthinkable 30 years ago, including criminalization and imprisonment, the prescription of psychotropic drugs, psychiatric confinement, and zero-tolerance policies that model schools after prisons. School has become a model for a punishing society in which children who violate a rule as minor as a dress code infraction or slightly act out in class can be handcuffed, booked, and jailed. Such was the case in Florida when the police handcuffed and arrested six-year-old Desré Watson, who was taken from her kindergarten school to the Highlander County jail where she was fingerprinted, photographed for a mug shot, and charged with a felony and two misdemeanors. Her crime? The six-year-old had thrown a tantrum in her class.[1] Couple this type of domestic terrorism with the fact that the United States is the only country that voted against a recent United Nations resolution calling for the abolition of life imprisonment without the possibility of parole for children under the age of 16 (Liptak 2007: A1). The United States is currently the only nation that locks up child offenders for life. A report issued in 2007 by the Equal Justice Initiative claims that "there are 73 Americans serving [life] sentences for crimes they committed at 13 or 14" (ibid.).

The attack on youth and its related effects are best exemplified in various representations of youth that shape the contemporary political landscape of American culture. Every society creates images and visions of those forces that threaten its existence, and how a society understands its youth is partly determined by how it represents them. Popular representations, in particular, constitute a cultural politics that shapes, mediates, and legitimates how adult society views youth and what it expects from them. Such representations produced and distributed through the mass media in sites such as television, video, music, film, publishing, and theater function as a form of **public pedagogy** actively attempting to define youth through the ideological filters of a society that is increasingly hostile to young people. All of these sites make competing claims on youth and their relation to the social order. At worst, they engage in a politics of representation, whether offered up in Hollywood films, television dramas, magazines, or popular advertisements, that constructs youth in terms that largely serve to demonize, sexualize, or commodify them, to reduce their sense of agency to the consumerist requirements of supply and demand. Such images not only resonate with larger public discourses that contribute to a moral panic about youth, but they also help to legitimate policies aimed at both containing and punishing young people, especially those who are marginalized by virtue of class, gender, race, and sexual orientation. At best, such representations define youth in complex ways that not only capture the problems, issues, and values that bear down on them, but also illustrate how varied youth in diverse circumstances attempt to negotiate the contradictions of a larger social order.

A society that represents children as a threat has no way of talking about the social contract or the future as central to a vibrant democracy. Moreover, such a society often finds it increasingly difficult to address the importance of those non-commodified

---

1 "Kindergarten Girl Handcuffed, Arrested at Fla. School," WFTV.com (March 30, 2007). Online: http://www.wftv.com/news/11455199/detail.html. For a more detailed examination of how schools have been modeled after prisons, see Robbins (2009) and Fuentes (2011).

values and public spaces that keep alive issues of justice, ethics, public opportunities, civic courage, and **critical citizenship**. In a society overrun by commercialism, it becomes difficult to find those public spheres where young people can locate metaphors of hope. The representation of youth in the United States suggests that the crisis of youth cannot be understood outside of the crisis of democracy, but at the same time such representations also point to the fact that the educational force of the culture constitutes one of the most important sites of learning in the 21st century. This is particularly true for those aspects of public space where teens and other youth learn how to define themselves outside of the traditional sites of instruction such as the home and the school. Learning in the postmodern age is located elsewhere—in popular spheres that shape their identities through forms of knowledge and desire that appear absent from what is taught in schools.[2] The literacies of the 21st century are electronic, aural, and image-based; and it is precisely within the diverse terrain of popular culture that pedagogical practices must be established as part of a broader politics of public life—practices that will aggressively subject dominant power to criticism, analysis, and transformation as part of a progressive reconstruction of democratic society. Images of youth, especially in popular culture, do not simply invoke a discourse of political and social responsibility, but also bear witness to a cultural politics in which the struggle over meaning is, in part, defined as the struggle over identity, agency, and power. And it is precisely in the name of such a struggle that images of youth must be constructed by, with, and for young people within public spheres that not only take democracy seriously, but also give substance to a future in which the lives of young people matter.

This book draws upon both theoretical resources and autobiographical memories to suggest how far rightward American political culture has shifted. What is ironically called free-market fundamentalism is really a form of **casino capitalism** that produces massive human suffering and hardships for both young people and adults. The struggles that youth face today, including class and racial oppression, the militarizing of schools, the criminalization of social problems, high rates of unemployment, soaring tuition costs, and the increasing burden of personal debt, cannot be limited to casino capitalism, but they are intensified by it. Moreover, the problems young people face are not just economic: they are cultural, social, and pedagogical.

Throughout the following chapters, I chart the war on youth, moving from my own memories of youth to the poisonous theater and culture of cruelty that now grip the United States in the first part of the 21st century. Central to this book is a language of both critique and hope. Not only do I point to specific problems, but I consistently gesture to historical and contemporary referents that offer a new language for struggle and social change, and accentuate the dialectical nature of pedagogy and the new

---

2 I have taken up this issue in a number of books. See, for example, Giroux (2001, 2004, 2009b), and Giroux and Searls Giroux (2004).

media and the potential role they might play in creating new social movements and modes of struggle. Most importantly, this book speaks to the need for young people to connect their private woes and troubles to public considerations and to organize collectively so as to be able not only to imagine otherwise but also to act otherwise. All around the globe young people are mobilizing, reclaiming the promise of democracy, and acting with a new sense of the power of their collective agency. In major cities around the United States, young people are protesting and taking aim at what they view as the criminal behavior of Wall Street, investors, corporations, banks, and other commanding institutions of the U.S. financial system. For example, the Occupy Wall Street protest movement is made up largely of young people who are using their collective voices to reclaim the promise of democracy and putting their bodies on the streets with the aim of creating the conditions for a renewed sense of hope along with the organizations that can begin to wage a successful struggle for a future very different from the one being offered to them today. Youth resistance has a long and dignified legacy in the United States. It is time to reclaim and intensify such struggles once again in the face of problems that, while dark and threatening, are far from being unsolvable. At stake here is not just the future of a new generation of young people, but democracy itself.

1: Youth in the Age of Moral and Political Plagues

s the 2010 health care debate made clear, the decades-long conservative campaign against the alleged abuses of "big government" is far from over. In the 1980s, when Ronald Reagan insisted that government was the problem, not the solution, he unleashed what was to become a **neoliberal** juggernaut against both the welfare state and the concept of the public good. Reagan's conservative ideological stance revealed a smoldering market-driven disdain for any form of governance that assumed a measure of responsibility for the education, health, and general welfare of the country's citizens. It also helped launch a new political era in which consumerism and profit-making were deemed to be the essence of democracy, and freedom was redefined as the unrestricted ability of markets to govern economic relations free of government regulation and practically without concern for ethical considerations and social costs. Even worse, the obligations of citizenship, if not agency itself, were reduced to the never-ending desire to consume goods, buy into market-driven services, and fashion public needs according to the protocols of celebrity culture.

For over 30 years, the American public has been reared on a **neoliberal** dystopian vision that legitimates itself through the largely unchallenged claim that there are no alternatives to a market-driven society, that economic growth should not be constrained by considerations of social costs or moral responsibility, and that democracy and capitalism are virtually synonymous. At the heart of this corporate-driven market rationality is an egocentric philosophy and culture of cruelty that sell off public goods and services to the corporate and private sectors while simultaneously dismantling those public spheres, social protections, and institutions serving the public good. As economic power increasingly frees itself from traditional government regulations, a new global financial class asserts the prerogatives of capital and proceeds to destroy systematically those public spheres advocating for social equality, along with the educated citizenry required for a viable democracy. At the same time, the corporate lobby for economic deregulation merges powerfully with the ideology of individual responsibility, effectively evading any notion of collective responsibility while undercutting any sense of corporate power's accountability to a broader public.

As the social contract comes under sustained attack, the bridges between public and private life are dismantled, and the corporate-dominated market or what I call

casino capitalism becomes a template for structuring all social relations. Democracy suffers a major hit, as public goods and institutions are sold off to the highest bidder.[1] The list of casualties is long and includes the ongoing privatization of public schools, health care, prisons, transportation, wars, the public airwaves, public lands, and other crucial elements of the commons, along with the undermining of many of our most basic civil liberties. At the same time, those institutions that once offered relief and hope to people are now replaced by the police, courts, and prisons, all of which have a disproportionately negative effect on poor and minority youth.[2] With the devaluing of public goods, public values, and public institutions, the model of the prison emerges as the primary mode of governance under the neoliberal state. As a result of the triumph of **corporate sovereignty** over democratic values, the supervisory authority of the state is reconfigured into a disciplinary device largely responsible for managing and expanding the mechanisms of control, containment, and punishment over a vast number of American institutions.

The legacy of casino capitalism, with its reckless gambling and corruption, has contributed to the loss of trillions of dollars from the public coffers while simultaneously undermining the most basic democratic values. Making a mockery of an aspiring American democracy, the **economic Darwinism** of the last 30 years has given free rein to a society that "celebrates fraud, theft, and violence" (Hedges 2009). The holy trinity of deregulation, privatization, and commodification has produced vast inequities in wealth, income, and power, exemplified by the fact that "at the start of the recession the collective wealth of the richest 1 percent of Americans was greater than that of the bottom 90 percent combined" (Herbert 2009: A19). But the regime of **free-market fundamentalism**—another term for casino capitalism—has not only produced "the biggest concentration of income and wealth since 1928" (Dreier 2007)[3]—it has also caused enormous hardship and suffering among those populations now considered redundant and increasingly disposable. Undeniably, the social and economic collapse we are now experiencing was preceded by a moral and political collapse, largely caused by an unscrupulous financial and political class and a **formative culture** deeply insensitive to social and ethical responsibilities. The renowned historian Tony Judt has insisted that since the 1980s we have inhabited what he calls "an age of pygmies," a time "consumed by locusts" and characterized by an "uncritical admiration for unfettered markets, disdain for the public sector, the delusion of

---

1 This new mode of political and economic authoritarianism can be found in Wolin (2008), Giroux (2008), and Hacker and Pierson (2010).

2 I develop this theme in great detail in Giroux (2009b).

3 As David R. Francis points out, "the richest of the rich, the top 1/1,000th, enjoyed a 497 percent gain in wage and salary income between 1972 and 2001. Those at the 99th percentile, who made an average $1.7 million per year in 2001, enjoyed a mere 181 percent gain" (Francis 2006).

endless growth … and an obsession with the pursuit of material wealth [while being] indifferent to so much else" (Judt 2010: 2, 39).

The dreamscape of **neoliberalism** has ushered in a long period of social and economic revenge against those populations marginalized by race and class. The new government of insecurity has reshaped welfare through punitive policies that criminalize poverty, push people into workfare programs so as to force them into menial labor, and use incarceration as the primary tool of making such populations disappear. As Loïc Wacquant has argued, "Poverty has not receded but the social visibility and civic standing of the trouble making poor have been reduced" (2009: 291). Moreover, we have witnessed in the last few decades the rise of a **punishing state** that "offers relief not to the poor but from the poor, by forcibly 'disappearing' the most disruptive of them, from the shrinking welfare rolls on the one hand, and into the swelling dungeons of the carceral castle on the other" (Wacquant 2009: 294). This is particularly true as more and more young people are caught in the punishing circuits of surveillance, containment, repression, and **disposability**. As a result of what can be called the war on youth, young people no longer are seen as part of the social contract and appear to have been banished from the everyday social investments, imagination, and future that once characterized the American dream.

Populations that were once viewed as facing dire problems in need of state interventions and social protections are now seen as a problem threatening society. This becomes clear when the war on poverty is transformed into a war against the poor— when young people, to paraphrase W. E. B. Du Bois, become problem people rather than people who face problems; when the plight of the homeless is defined less as a political and economic issue in need of social reform than as a matter of law and order; and when state budgets for prison construction eclipse budgets for higher education. The reach of the punishing state is especially evident in the ways in which many public schools now use punishment as the main tool for control. In the devalued landscape of public schooling, what becomes clear is that disciplining young people seems to be far more important than educating them (Eckholm 2010b: A14). Similarly, as advocates of market rationality raise an entire generation on the alleged virtues of "unrestricted individual responsibility," the disdain towards the common good finds its counterpart in increasing acts of "collective and political irresponsibility" (Wacquant 2009: 6).

What might it mean to oppose the institutions, reverse the values, and challenge the power relations that created this theater of civic morbidity and culture of cruelty? Dare one not take account of the profound emotional appeal, let alone ideological hold, of neoliberalism on the American public? The success of a market ideology that has produced shocking levels of inequality, poverty, and human suffering buttressed by a market morality that has spawned rapacious greed and corruption should raise fundamental questions. For example, the United States has over 50 million people living in poverty—including 16.4 million children—and over 50 million without health care. All the while, in the midst of such deprivation, the top 1 percent of the population control 40 percent of the nation's wealth and take home 25 percent of the national income. How did market rule prove capable of enlisting in such a compelling way the consent of the vast majority of Americans, who cast themselves, no less, in the role of the "moral majority"? This means the questions we need to be asking ourselves must extend beyond how we proceed with competent and effective economic reform. Just as neoliberal logic extends well beyond the economic realm, we must also consider at a deeper level how we dismantle the culture of permanent war, fraud, cruelty, and fear; how we learn to think beyond the narrow dictates of **instrumental rationalities**; how we de-criminalize certain identities; how we de-pathologize the concept of dependency and recognize it as our common fate; how we foster a culture of questioning and shared responsibilities; how we reclaim the public good—how we reconstitute, in short, a viable, sustainable, and aspiring democratic society. What are the implications of theorizing education, justice, and the practice of learning as essential to social change, and where might such interventions take place? One such place to begin, especially for educators, is with the current state of young people in the United States.

While youth have always represented an ambiguous category, young people are under assault today in ways that are entirely new because they now face a world that is far more dangerous than at any other time in recent history. As Jean-Marie Durand points out, when war and the criminalization of social problems become a mode of governance, "Youth is no longer considered the world's future, but as a threat to its present. [For] youth, there is no longer any political discourse except for a disciplinary one" (Durand 2009). In the current historical moment, young people are increasingly defined through a **youth crime-control complex** that is predatory in nature and punishing in its consequences, leaving a generation of young people with damaged lives, impoverished spirits, and bankrupted hopes. This intensifying assault on young people can be more fully grasped through what I have called in the past the related concepts of "soft war" and "hard war" (see Giroux 2009b).

The soft war refers to the changing conditions of youth within the relentless expansion of a global consumer society that devalues and exploits all youth by treating them as markets or as **commodities** themselves. This low-intensity war is waged through the educational force of a culture that not only commercializes every aspect of kids' lives but also uses the Internet, cell phones, and various social networks along with the new media technologies to address young people as markets and consumers in ways that are more direct and expansive. The reach of the new screen and electronic culture on young people is disturbing. For instance, a recent study by the Kaiser Family Foundation found that "young people ages 8 to 18 are spending more than seven and a half hours a day with smart phones, computers, television, and other electronic devices, compared with less than six and a half hours five years ago" (Lewin 2010: A1). When you add the additional time youth spend texting, talking on their cell phones, "watching TV while updating Facebook—the number rises to 11 hours of total media content each day" (Christine 2010). There is more at stake here than what some call a new form of attention deficit disorder, one in which youth avoid the time necessary for thoughtful analysis and engaged modes of reading. There is also the issue of how these media are being used to create a new generation of consuming subjects. Corporations have hit gold with the new media and can inundate young people directly with market-driven values, desires, and identities, all of which are removed from the mediation and watchful eyes of parents and other adults.

The hard war is more serious and dangerous for young people and refers to the harshest elements, values, and dictates of a growing youth crime-control complex that increasingly governs poor minority youth through a logic of punishment, surveillance, and control. For example, the imprint of the youth crime-control complex is evident in the increasingly popular practice of organizing schools through disciplinary practices that subject them to constant surveillance through high-tech security technologies while imposing upon them harsh and often thoughtless zero-tolerance policies that closely resemble the culture of prisons. In this instance, even as the corporate state is in financial turmoil, it is transformed into a punishing state, and certain segments of the youth population become the object of a new mode of governance based on the crudest forms of disciplinary control. Many poor minority youth are not just excluded from "the American dream" but are treated as utterly redundant and disposable—waste products of a society that no longer considers them of any value. Such youth now experience a kind of social death as they are pushed out of schools, denied job-training opportunities, subjected to rigorous modes of surveillance and criminal sanctions, and viewed less as disadvantaged than as flawed consumers and civic felons. Under such circumstances, matters of survival and **disposability** become central to how we think about and imagine not just politics but the everyday existence of poor white and minority youth.

As the social safety net and protections unraveled in the last 30 years, the culture and administrative apparatus of the prison, operating within the narrow registers of punishment and crime management, emerged as a core institution of American society. In part, this is evident in the fact that over seven million people are now under the jurisdiction of some element of the criminal justice system. Within this regime of harsh disciplinary control, there is no political or moral vocabulary either for recognizing the systemic economic, social, and educational problems that young people face or for addressing what it means for American society to invest seriously in the future of young people, especially poor minority and white youth. Instead of being viewed as impoverished, minority youth are seen as lazy and shiftless; instead of being understood in terms of how badly they are served by failing schools, many poor minority youth are labeled as uneducable and pushed out of education, or even worse. Against the idealistic rhetoric of a nation that claims it venerates young people lies the reality of a society that increasingly views youth through the optic of law and order and that is all too willing to treat them as criminals, and, when necessary, make them "disappear" into the farthest reaches of the **carceral state**.

What are we to make of a society that allows the police to come into a school and arrest, handcuff, and haul off a 12-year-old student for doodling on her desk? Even worse, where is the public outrage over a school system that allows a six-year-old kindergarten pupil to be handcuffed and sent to a hospital psychiatric ward for being unruly in a classroom? What does it mean when a society looks the other way as 25 Chicago middle-schoolers ranging in age from 11 to 15 years old are arrested for a food fight, held for 11 hours at the police station, charged with misdemeanor reckless conduct, and later suspended from school for two days? Or when an 11-year-old autistic and cognitively impaired child is repeatedly abused in school by both teachers and security guards (Germano 2010)? Where is the public outrage when the mainstream media report on two officers called to a daycare center in central Indiana to handle an unruly 10-year-old and one of the officers ends up using a stun gun on the boy while his partner slaps him in the mouth? Or when a police officer in Arkansas uses a stun gun on a girl of the same age? One response reported in the media came from Steve Tuttle, a spokesman for Taser International Inc., who insisted that a "stun gun can be safely used on children" (Everson 2010). Sadly, this is a small sampling of the ways in which children are being punished instead of educated in American schools. All of these examples point to how little regard our society has for young people and the growing number of institutions willing to employ a crime-and-punishment mentality. We are witnessing social and cultural change that constitutes not only a crisis of politics, but the emergence of new politics of educating and governing through crime (Simon 2007: 5).

The abuse of children in and out of schools has become endemic to American society, and the culture of cruelty that produces it is increasingly being mimicked by the children who are subject to it daily. Violence, harsh modes of competition, a crippling emphasis on toughness—all coupled with stripped-down forms of pedagogy that confuse training with education—leave young people unprepared to resist enacting the worst dimensions of the selfish, narcissistic values and behaviors that dominate a celebrity-infatuated consumer society. This moral and political tragedy is made obvious by the many "get-tough" policies that have rendered young people as criminals, while depriving them of basic conditions necessary to improve the quality of their lives and future. At the same time, the influence of such policies on the behavior of young people can be seen in the rise of bullying and violence they increasingly inflict on each other. As Christopher Robbins has written in his eloquent book *Expelling Hope*, punishment and fear have replaced compassion and social responsibility as the most important modalities mediating the relationship of youth not only to the larger social order but also to each other. Subject to a coming-of-age crisis marked by an ever-expanding police order with its paranoid machinery of security, containment, and criminalization, many young people are removed from modes of education that should provide them with the knowledge and skills necessary for them to think critically about education, justice, and democracy.

At this moment in history, it is more necessary than ever to register youth as a central theoretical, moral, and political concern. Doing so reminds adults of their ethical and political responsibility to future generations. It also legitimates both a symbolic and an actual investment in youth and democracy by nurturing civic imagination, critical thinking, and collective resistance in response to the suffering of others. Youth provide a powerful referent for a discussion about the long-term consequences of neoliberal policies, while also gesturing towards the need for putting into place those economic, political, and cultural institutions that make a democratic future possible.

One way of addressing our collapsing intellectual and moral visions regarding young people is to imagine those policies, values, opportunities, and social relations that both invoke adult responsibility and reinforce the ethical imperative to provide young people, especially those marginalized by race and class, with the economic, social, and educational conditions that make life livable and the future sustainable. Clearly, the issue at stake here is not a one-off bailout or temporary fix, but real, structural reforms. At the very least, this suggests fighting for a child welfare system that would reduce "family poverty by increasing the minimum wage," and mobilizing for legislation that would institute "a guaranteed income, provide high-quality subsidized child care, preschool education, and paid parental leaves for all families" (Roberts 2008: 268). Young people need a federally funded jobs-creation program and wage subsidy that would provide year-round employment for out-of-school youth and summer jobs that assist in-school, low-income youth. Public and higher education, increasingly shaped by corporate and instrumental values, must be reclaimed as **democratic public spheres** committed to teaching young people about how to govern rather than merely be governed. Incarceration should be the last resort, not the preferred option, for dealing with our children. Any viable notion of educational reform must include equitable funding schemes for schools, reinforced by the recognition that the problems facing public schools cannot be solved with corporate solutions or law-enforcement strategies. We need to get the police out of public schools, greatly reduce spending for prisons and military expenditures, and hire more teachers, support staff, and community people in order to eliminate the **school-to-prison pipeline**.

In order to make life livable for young people and others, basic supports must be put in place, such as a system of national health insurance that covers everybody, along with provisions for affordable housing. At the very least, we need to lower the age of eligibility for Medicare to 55 in order to keep poor families from going bankrupt. And, of course, none of this will take place unless the institutions, social relations, and values that legitimate and reproduce current levels of inequality, power, and human suffering are dismantled. The widening gap between the rich and the poor has to be addressed if young people are to have a viable future. And that requires pervasive structural reforms that constitute a real shift in power and politics away from a market-driven system that views too many children as disposable. We need to reimagine what liberty, equality, and freedom might mean as truly democratic values and practices.

As public life is commercialized, commodified, and policed, the pathology of individual entitlement and narcissism erodes those public spaces in which the conditions for conscience, decency, self-respect, and dignity take root. The crisis of youth is symptomatic of the current crisis of democracy, and as such it hails us as much for the threat that it poses as for the challenges and possibilities it invokes. We need to liberate the discourse and spaces of freedom from the plague of consumer narcissism and casino capitalism. We need to engage the struggle to restore and build those public spaces where democratic ideals, visions, and social relations can be nurtured and developed as part of a genuinely meaningful education and politics. The time has come to take seriously the words of the great abolitionist Frederick Douglass, who bravely argued that freedom is an empty abstraction if people fail to act. Douglass insisted that "If there is no struggle there is no progress. Those who profess to favor freedom and yet depreciate agitation, are men [and women] who want crops without plowing up the ground, they want rain without thunder and lightning. They want the ocean without the awful roar of its many waters" (Douglass 1985: 204).

The deteriorating state of American youth, especially poor white and minority youth, may be the most serious challenge the United States will face in the 21st century. It is a struggle that demands a new understanding of politics, one that is infused not only with the language of critique, but also with the discourse of possibility. It is a struggle that requires us to think beyond the given, imagine the unimaginable, and combine the lofty ideals of democracy with a willingness to fight for its realization. But this is not a fight we can win through individual struggles or isolated political movements. It demands new modes of solidarity, new political organizations, and a powerful, expansive social movement capable of uniting diverse political interests and groups. It is a struggle that is as educational as it is political, one that must build upon self-awareness as well as historical consciousness. At the present moment, it is a struggle whose call for reflection and action is as necessary as it is urgent. Those of us who believe in justice and human rights need to liberate the discourse and spaces of freedom from the plagues of militarism and consumer narcissism and struggle to build those public spaces where democratic ideals, visions, and social relations can be nurtured and developed as part of a genuinely meaningful education and politics—we need along with young people to build those spaces, social relations, and institutions that give meaning to both the promise of democracy and a future in which young people matter.

II: Memories of Hope and Youth in the Age of Disposability

Any rigorous conception of youth must take into account the inescapable intersection of the personal, social, political, and pedagogical embodied by young people. Beneath the abstract codifying of youth around the discourses of law, medicine, psychology, employment, education, and marketing statistics, there is the lived experience of being young. For me, youth invokes a repository of memories fueled by my own journey through an adult world that largely seemed to be in the way, a world held together by a web of disciplinary practices and restrictions that appeared at the time more oppressive than liberating. Lacking the security of a middle-class childhood, my friends and I seemed suspended in a society that neither accorded us a voice nor guaranteed economic independence. Identity didn't come easy in my neighborhood. It was painfully clear to all of us that our identities were constructed out of daily battles waged around masculinity, the ability to mediate a terrain fraught with violence, and the need to find an anchor through which to negotiate a culture in which life was fast and short-lived. I grew up amid the motion and force of mostly working-class male bodies—bodies asserting their physical strength as one of the few resources we had control over.

Dreams for the youth of my Smith Hill neighborhood in Providence, Rhode Island, were contained within a limited number of sites, all of which occupied an outlaw status in the adult world: the inner-city basketball court located in a housing project, which promised danger and fierce competition; the streets on which adults and youth collided as the police and parole officers harassed us endlessly; the New York System hole-in-the-wall restaurant operated by a guy who always had 10 hot dogs and buns in various stages of preparation on his arm on a Saturday night and would wait for us to do business after we spent a night hanging out, drinking, and dancing.

For many of the working-class youth in my neighborhood, the basketball court was one of the few public spheres in which the kind of **cultural capital** we recognized and took seriously could be exchanged for respect and admiration. If you weren't good enough, you didn't play; if you were good, you performed with a kind of humility arbitrated by a code that suggested you didn't lose easily. Nobody was born with innate talent. Nor was anybody given instant recognition. The basketball court became for me a rite of passage and a powerful referent for developing a sense of possibility. We played day and night, and we played in any space that was available. Even when we got caught breaking into St. Patrick's Elementary School one Friday night around one o'clock in the morning, the cops who found us knew we were there to play basketball rather than to steal money from the teachers' rooms or the vending machines. Basketball was taken very seriously because it was a neighborhood sport, a terrain where respect was earned. It offered us a mode of resistance, if not a respite, from the lure of drug dealing, the sport of everyday violence, and the general misery that surrounded us. The basketball court provided another kind of hope, one that seemed to fly in the face of the need for high status, school credentials, or the security of a boring job. It was also a sphere in which we learned about the value of friendship, solidarity, and respect for the other.

Yet the promise of the basketball court evaporated when high school ended, and all but a talented few of the young men in the neighborhood moved from school to any one of a number of dead-end jobs, or public service work that offered a more promising future. The best opportunities came from taking a civil service test, and if one were lucky one got a job as a policeman or fireman (as James Brown reminded us, it was strictly a "man's world" then). Job or no job, one forever felt the primacy of the body: the body flying through the rarefied air of the neighborhood gym in a kind of sleek and stylized performance; the body furtive and cool existing on the margins of society filled with the possibility of instant pleasure and relief, or tense and anticipating the danger and risk; the body bent by the weight of grueling labor.

The body, with its **fugitive** status within middle-class culture, allowed boys like myself from white, working-class neighborhoods to cross racial borders and rewrite the endemic racism of our community. We were white boys, and race and class positioned our bodies in turf wars marked by street codes that were both feared and respected. At the age of eight, I became a shoeshine boy and staked out a route inhabited by black and white nightclubs in Providence. On Thursday, Friday, and Saturday nights I started my route at seven o'clock and got home around midnight. I loved going into the Celebrity Club and other bars, watching the adults dance, drink, and steal furtive glances from each other. Most of all I loved the music. Billie Holiday, Fats Domino, Dinah Washington, Frankie Lymon and the Teenagers, and Little Richard played in the background against the sounds of glasses clinking and men and women talking—talking as if their only chance to come alive was compressed into the time they spent in the club. Whenever I finished my route, I had to navigate a dangerous set of streets to get back home. I learned how to talk, negotiate, and defend myself along that route. I was too skinny as a kid to be a tough guy; I had to learn a street code that was funny but smart, fast but not insulting. That's when my body and head started working together. While I didn't realize it at the time, I was learning quickly that the intellect was as powerful a weapon as the body itself. In spite of what I learned in that neighborhood about the virtues of a kind of militant masculinity, I had to forge a different understanding about the relationship between my body and mind—one in which the body was only one resource for surviving.

I saw a lot in that neighborhood, and I couldn't seem to learn enough to make sense of it or escape its pull. Peer groups formed early, and kids ruptured all but the most necessary forms of dependence on their parents at a very young age. I really only saw my parents when I went home to eat or sleep. All of the youth I grew up with left home too early to notice the loss until later in life when we became adults or parents ourselves. Leaving home for me was made all the more complicated because my mother had severe epilepsy and had repeated seizures. My sister and I were not distant observers to my mother's suffering—we often had to hold her down in bed when the seizures erupted. Shuffled between hospitals and institutions, my mother wasn't home much. As a result of my mother's absence, my sister was taken away by the social services and placed in a Catholic residence for girls. Losing my sister to an orphanage, I experienced for the first time what it meant to be homeless in my own home. Home was neither a source of comfort nor a respite from the outside world. The neighborhood was my real home, and my friends provided the sanctuary for talk and security, along with a cool indifference to the fact that none of us looked forward to the future. When I was in high school, I remember visiting my mother in state hospitals and being alarmed by the fact that many of the attendants were guys from my neighborhood, guys who seemed dangerous and utterly indifferent to human life, guys whom on the streets I had both known and avoided. It seemed to me like everybody was warehoused in that neighborhood, irrespective of age.

I eventually left my neighborhood, but it was nothing less than a historical accident that allowed me to leave. I never took the requisite tests to apply to a four-year college. When high school graduation came around, I was offered a basketball scholarship to a junior college in Worcester, Massachusetts. It seemed better to me than working in a factory, so I went off to school with few expectations and no plans except to play ball. I was placed in a business program but had no interest in what the program offered. The culture of the college seemed terribly alien to me, and I missed my old neighborhood. After violating too many rules and drinking more than I should have, I saw clearly that my life had reached an impasse. I left school and went back to my old neighborhood hangouts.

My friends' lives had already changed. Their youth had left them, and they now had families and lousy jobs and spent a lot of time in the neighborhood bar waiting for a quick hit at the racetrack or the promise of a good disability scheme. After working for two years at odd jobs, I managed to play in the widely publicized Fall River basketball tournament and did well enough to attract the attention of a few coaches who tried to recruit me. Following their advice, I took the SATs and scored high enough to qualify for entrance into a small college in Maine that offered me a basketball scholarship. But nothing came easy for me when it involved school. Although I made the starting lineup on the varsity team and managed to be the team high-scorer in my freshman year, the coach resented me because I was an urban kid—too flashy, too hip, and maybe too dangerous for the rural town of Gorham, Maine. I left the team at the beginning of my sophomore year, took on a couple of jobs to finance my education, and eventually graduated with a teaching degree in secondary education.

After getting my teaching certificate, I became a community organizer and a high school teacher. Then, worn thin after six years of teaching high school social studies, I applied for and received another scholarship, this one to attend Carnegie Mellon University. I finished my course work early and spent a year unemployed while writing my dissertation. While at Carnegie Mellon I worked with a wonderful professor named Tony Penna, who eventually became my advisor. Whatever I knew about progressive and critical education at that point I learned from him. He was an excellent mentor and a great friend. I finally got a job at Boston University. Again, politics and culture worked their strange magic as I taught, published, and prepared for tenure. My tenure experience changed my perception of liberalism forever. Like many idealistic young academics, I believed that if I worked hard at teaching and publishing I would surely get tenure. I did my best to follow the rules, but did so with little understanding of the political forces governing Boston University at that time. It turned out I was dead wrong about the rules and the alleged integrity of the tenure process.

By the time I came up for tenure review, I had published two books and fifty journal articles and given numerous talks, and I went through the tenure process unanimously at every level of the university. But then, unexpectedly, I was denied tenure by the then president of Boston University, who not only ignored the tenure committee recommendations but actually solicited letters supporting denial of my tenure from notable conservatives. One review was embarrassing in that it began with the comment, "I have read all of the work of Robert Giroux." One of my supporters at the university threatened to resign if I did not receive tenure. Of course, he didn't. The actions of the man denying my tenure had a chilling effect on many faculty members who had initially rallied to my support. They realized quickly that the tenure process was a rigged affair under his regime and that anyone who complained about it might compromise his or her own academic career. One faculty member apologized to me for his refusal to meet with the man in question to protest my tenure decision. Arguing that he owned two condos in the city, he explained that he couldn't afford to act on his conscience since he would be risking his investments. Of course, his conscience went on vacation when it came to acting in defense of his material assets.

By the time I met this man to discuss my case, I was convinced that my fate had already been decided. He met me in his office, asked me why I wrote such "shit," and made me an offer. He suggested that if I studied the philosophy of science and logic with him as my personal tutor, I could maintain my current salary and would be reconsidered for tenure in two years. The only other catch was that I had to agree not to write or publish anything during that time. I was taken aback, and responded with a joke by asking him if he wanted to turn me into well-known conservative journalist George Will. He missed the humor, and I left. I declined the offer, was denied tenure, and after sending off numerous applications finally landed a job at Miami University.

Working-class intellectuals do not fare well in the culture of higher education, especially when they are on the left of the political spectrum. I have been asked many times since this incident whether I would have continued the critical writing that has marked my career if I had known that I was going to be fired because of the ideological orientation of my work. Needless to say, for me, it is better to live standing up than on one's knees. Sadly, my story of being denied tenure at Boston University—at the time an aberration from the norm—is now becoming an all-too-familiar tale. Today, academics have become another group suffering from the threat of exclusion and **disposability** as their autonomy is increasingly questioned and constrained by business-oriented administrators. Most faculty members today are not even given the opportunity to get tenure in this new age of casino capitalism. Over 70 percent of faculty members now find themselves part of a subaltern class of part-time and contingent labor without any power or collective representation. Hence, many of them are too frightened to speak out or address important social issues in their classroom for fear of being fired.

In my early career at the university, the academic game seemed to be rigged against me, but even then I had become more of an exception than the rule. The lesson here is that whether we are talking about failure or success, surely the experiences of many working-class kids in this culture are more an effect of their place in society than the result of either personal inadequacy, on the one hand, or an unswerving commitment to the ethic of hard work and individual responsibility on the other.

My youth was lived through class formations that I felt were largely viewed by others as an outlaw culture. Schools, hospitals, community centers, and surely middle-class social spaces interpreted us as alien, other, and deviant because we were from the wrong class and had the wrong kind of cultural capital. As working-class youth, we were defined through our deficits. Class marked us as poor, inferior, linguistically inadequate, and often dangerous. Our bodies were more valued than our minds, and the only way to survive was to deny our voices, experiences, and location as working-class youth. We were feared and denigrated more than we were affirmed, and the reality of being part of an outlaw culture penetrated us with an awareness that we could hardly navigate critically or theoretically, but still felt in every fiber of our being.

The working-class culture in which I grew up wore its fugitive status like a badge, but all too often it was unaware of the contradictions that gave it meaning. We lacked the political vocabulary and insight that would have enabled us to see the contradiction between the brutal racism, violence, and sexism that marked our lives and our constant attempts to push against the grain by investing in the pleasures of body, the warmth of solidarity, and the appropriation of neighborhood spaces as outlaw publics. As kids, we were **border crossers** and had to learn to negotiate the power, violence, and cruelty of the dominant culture through our own lived histories, restricted languages, and narrow cultural experiences. Recognizing our fugitive status in all of the dominant institutions in which we found ourselves—including schools, the workplace, and social services—we were suspicious and sometimes vengeful of what we didn't have or how we were left out of the representations that seemed to define American youth in the 1950s and early 1960s. We listened to Etta James and hated both the music of Pat Boone and the cultural capital that for us was synonymous with golf, tennis, and prep schools. We lost ourselves in the grittiness of working-class neighborhood gyms, abandoned cars, and street corners that offered a haven for escape, but also invited police surveillance and brutality. Being part of an **outlaw culture** meant that we lived almost exclusively on the margins of a life that was not of our choosing. And as for the present, it was all we had, since it made no sense to invest in a future that for many of my friends either ended too early or pointed to the dreaded possibility of becoming an adult, which usually meant working in a boring job by day and hanging out in the local bar by night. We bore witness to the future only to escape into the present, and the present never stopped pulsating. Like most marginalized youth cultures, we were time-bound. The memory-work would have to come later. But when it came it offered us a newfound appreciation of what we learned in those neighborhoods about solidarity, trust, friendship, sacrifice, and, most of all, individual and collective struggle.

Bearing **witness** as I have tried to do is not simply an autobiographical rendering of personal events. It is a mode of analysis that seeks to connect private troubles to larger social forces, just as it always implicates one's self in a collective past. Connecting my own story to an awareness of broader social issues gives rise to reflections on how youth act and are acted upon within a myriad of public sites, cultures, and institutions. Some theorists have suggested that the practices of **witnessing** and **testimony** lie at the heart of what it means to teach and to learn. Witnessing and testimony, translated here, mean speaking and listening to the stories of others as part of both an ethical response to the narratives of the past and a moral responsibility to engage the present. I often wonder how my own formation as a working-class youth and eventual border crosser, moving often without an "official passport" between cultures, ideologies, jobs, and fugitive knowledge, might be invoked as a form of bearing witness. How might the testimony to which I bear witness help me not only to interrogate my own shifting location as a critical educator, but also provide an important narrative and locus for identification through which others can begin to understand the complexity and significance of the different conditions that have shaped our individual and collective histories? The message for educators and other cultural workers that emerges out of this engagement is the pedagogical challenge that "if teaching does not hit upon some sort of crisis, if it does not encounter either the vulnerability or the explosiveness of a[n] (explicit or implicit) critical and unpredictable dimension, it has perhaps not truly taught" (Felman and Laub 1992: 53).

The crisis I speak of in this instance is about the plight of youth as a social and political category in an age of increasing symbolic, material, and institutional violence. It is a crisis rooted in society's loss of any sense of history, memory, and ethical responsibility. The ideas of the public good, the notion of connecting learning to social change, the idea of civic courage being infused by social justice, have been lost in an age of rabid consumerism, media-induced spectacles, and short-term, high-yield financial investments. Under the regime of a rigidly market-driven society, concepts and practices of community and solidarity have been replaced by a world of cutthroat survival, even as politics has become an extension of war. What youth learn quickly today is that their fate is solely a matter of individual survival, a natural law of sorts that has more to do with survival instinct than with modes of collective reasoning, social solidarity, and the formation of a sustainable democratic society.

My youth may be marked as the last time when young people could still experience the hope and support given to poor youth in the form of a social state that took the social contract seriously. While we may have lived in private hells, we never felt entirely demonized or shut out from the most basic social services. Nor did we feel that our troubles were simply private issues. We hung out at the boys' club, took part in after-school sports, joined summer leagues, had an opportunity to attend day camps, and knew that even in the worst of times we could count on (in the present and in the future) medical services, a job, and a wage, however unfair. Politicians at either end of the political spectrum viewed youth as a social investment, even if it meant investing in some youth more than in others. Responsibility both provided moral sustenance and presented occasions in which the practices of compassion, trust, and respect mediated the relationship between the self and others. Authority was never beyond critique; resistance was a mark of pride; and the moral obligation to care for others was embodied in our personal codes, religious institutions, and state-sponsored services. A respect for the common good prevailed. Community was a word, however flawed, that resonated with a deeply felt concern for the public good and the public institutions that nourished it. Love, friendship, hard work, helping neighbors in distress, and respect for the people one associated with thrived in that neighborhood where I grew up. Labels and logos did not define my generation. Commodity culture was outside of our reach, and it was only later in life that I realized what a blessing that had been, growing up in a neighborhood organized around a different and more honest set of values in which the suffering and misfortunes of others were taken seriously.

What was striking about my Smith Hill neighborhood was the view that nobody was disposable and that giving and receiving collective support was a virtue, not a liability or a sign of weakness. In the midst of poverty and various crisis situations, the entire working-class neighborhood often mobilized to provide food, clothing, and, in some cases, money for distressed families and disadvantaged young people. The men and women in my neighborhood worked hard, shared their stories, gathered at church on Sundays, and recognized injustice when they saw it. Very few people back then bought into the myth that individuals alone had to bear both the blame and the responsibility for their own survival in times of crisis. If the parents, young people, and working-class adults I grew up with lacked power, they made up for it by working hard within the limits imposed on them in a society that produced vast amounts of inequality and brutality.

Youth in my neighborhood had a difficult time growing up. There were no innocent young people on those streets, just young people trying to act like adults in order to stay alive and get by. But in spite of how bad it was, there was a sense of civic values and a respect for the public good that all of us believed in. If youth were under siege, it was largely because of repressive forces that were imposed on us from alien and hostile sites that we tried to stay clear of. The police roamed our neighborhoods on foot patrols, and, while often repressive and **authoritarian**, they were still absent from our schools. When we went to school, we didn't have to face the disciplinary apparatus of an expanding criminal justice system that many young people face today with the ongoing development of a youth crime-control complex and militarized schools. We were disciplined in a much different manner. Guidance teachers were the masters of our fate and shamelessly determined how many of us poor kids should be in vocational classes because we were clearly incapable of being intelligent. But there were no police in my school, just adult authority figures and teachers who believed that the school was a public rather than a private good, however flawed their actions were at times. While many of us were tracked at Hope High School by administrators and teachers who felt we were more of a liability than an asset, there were also plenty of other adults around to offer guidance and help. They picked us up and gave us a ride to school on occasion, given the long hike and often inclement weather we had to face. They often lived in our neighborhoods and knew people in the community. They joked with us, understood the restricted code, and watched out for those young people who were always on the verge of dropping out of high school. If it hadn't been for one particular guidance teacher and a coach named Leo DiMaeo, I never would have thought about going to college.

In the 1950s and 60s, the neoliberal world of vast inequalities and exclusions in which people are only connected to each other through the possibility of enhancing profit margins was only just beginning to reveal its ugly values and institutional tentacles. Matters of agency and politics, however deformed, were still the subject and grounds for both criticism and hope. Collective responsibility for individual well-being was still alive, at least as an ideal, in the America of my youth, and it was precisely such an ideal that drove the civil rights movement, the student rebellions of the sixties, and the Great Society policies under President Lyndon Johnson. Put another way, a democratic consciousness at that point in history had not been snuffed out by market-driven values and policies mobilized under the reign of a cruel and unjust neoliberalism, largely hatched among the elite at the University of Chicago and in the highest levels of government.[1] Privatized utopias and gated spaces were not part of our experience as young people growing up at that time. The consumerist utopia that would later descend like a plague on American society in the late 1970s and 1980s was still capable of being challenged and resisted in the search for more democratic and compassionate values and social relations.

For many poor white youth and youth of color today, the notion of solidarity and the sense of dependence and respect that marked my childhood are gone. Instead, America is waging not only an immoral and unjust war abroad in Iraq and Afghanistan, but also a more insidious, high-intensity war at home against any viable notion of the social.[2] Social protections and investments, even as they apply to youth who are utterly dependent upon the larger society, are now objects of scorn as right-wing politicians—whom I call the new barbarians—demand the elimination of Medicare, Medicaid, Social Security, unemployment benefits, and any other program aimed at helping those suffering from the systemic failures of an unjust and often cruel socioeconomic system. For many young people today, the possibility of a better future has vanished, as one in seven Americans lives in poverty and over fifty million are deprived of health insurance.[3] More and more children are growing up poor, facing a world with few job opportunities, and viewed as being trouble rather than facing troubles. Food banks and prisons have become the new public spheres for young Americans who are poor and marginalized. As poverty reaches record levels, the number of children in poverty has risen to 15.5 million, and there is barely a peep of outrage heard from either politicians and intellectuals or the general public.

When the anti-youth and conservative politicians suggest that young people get married in order to avoid poverty, the statement is analyzed by mainstream media and anti-public intellectuals less as a lapse into savagery than as a thoughtful policy suggestion (Goldstein 2010). Rather than call for policies that could keep young Americans out of poverty, such as combating rising income inequality and providing more jobs and benefits for the growing multitude of disposable youth and adults, the right-wing barbarians talk about how the Obama administration is abusing the rich and powerful by refusing to extend the tax breaks given to them by George W. Bush. The new barbarians' vitriolic outrage over the deficit and government spending is utterly hypocritical and ideologically transparent as they simultaneously argue for extending

---

1 On the history and rationality of neoliberalism, see the excellent work by David Harvey: for instance, *A Brief History of Neoliberalism* (2005) and *The Enigma of Capital and the Crisis of Capitalism* (2010). See also Giroux (2008).

2 For a brilliant analysis and critique of Bush's and Obama's wars in Iraq and Afghanistan, see the various books by Andrew Bacevich, particularly *Washington Rules: America's Path to Permanent War* (2010), and *Limits of Power* (2009).

3 Figures on the new poverty levels and other indexes of misfortune can be found in Morello (2010), Eckholm (2010a), and Child Trends (2010).

high-end tax breaks for the rich and powerful—a move that will deprive the government of over $700 billion in much-needed revenue. Lost in their discourse is any attempt to reflect on failed right-wing policies that spawned the economic recession in the first place. And there is certainly little attempt on the part of conservative Republican and Democratic Party members to champion policies that might actually "expand the safety net, strengthen labor rights, build a more humane and efficient health care system, reward hard work with living wages, and value society's most vulnerable members, children" (Shakir et al. 2010).

The new culture of cruelty combines with the arrogance of the rich as morally bankrupt politicians such as Mike Huckabee tell his fellow Republican extremists that the provision in Obama's health care bill that requires insurance companies to cover people with pre-existing conditions should be repealed because people who have these conditions are like houses that have already burned down. The metaphor is apt in a country that no longer has a language for compassion, justice, and social responsibility. Huckabee is at least honest about one thing. He makes clear that the right-wing fringe leading the Republican Party is on a death march and has no trouble endorsing policies in which millions of people—in this case those afflicted by illness—can simply "dig their own graves and lie down in them."[4] Killing is one of the preferred methods of cruelty, and acceptance, even glorification, of killing was evident recently, soon after Osama bin Laden was assassinated by American forces. As Jonathan Schell points out, bin Laden's death "touched off raucous celebrations around the country. It is one thing to believe in the unfortunate necessity of killing someone, another to revel in it. This is especially disturbing when it is not only government officials but ordinary people who engage in the effusions" (Schell 2011). The politics of disposability ruthlessly puts money and profits ahead of human needs. Under the rubric of austerity, the new barbarians such as Huckabee and Ron Paul now advocate eugenicist policies in which people who are considered weak, sick, disabled, or suffering from debilitating health conditions are targeted to be weeded out and removed from the body politic and social safety nets that any decent society puts into place to ensure that everyone, but especially the most disadvantaged, can access decent health care and lead a life with dignity.

Former Vice-President, Dick Cheney, publicly admits and defends the use of state torture. Cruelty, in this instance, suggests not only dark times, as Hannah Arendt once wrote, but points to a society sinking into an authoritarian nightmare. Under such circumstances, politics loses its democratic character along with any sense of responsibility and becomes part of a machinery of violence that mimics the fascistic policies of past authoritarian political parties that eagerly attempted to purify their

---

4 See William Rivers Pitt's passionate and insightful commentary on Huckabee's comments and how politically and morally bankrupt they are in Pitt (2010).

societies by getting rid of those human beings considered weak and inferior, and who were ultimately viewed as human waste. I don't think it is an exaggeration to say that a lunatic fringe of a major political party is shamelessly mimicking and nourishing the barbaric roots of one of the most evil periods in human history. By arguing that individuals with pre-existing health conditions are like burned down houses who do not deserve health insurance, Huckabee puts into place those forces and ideologies that allow the country to move closer to the end point of such logic by suggesting that such disposable populations do not deserve to live at all.

Welcome to the new era of disposability in which market-driven values peddle policies that promote massive amounts of human suffering and death for millions of human beings. Programs to help the elderly, middle-aged, and youth overcome poverty, get decent jobs, obtain access to health insurance and decent health care, and exercise their dignity and rights as American citizens are denounced in the name of austerity measures that only apply to those who are not rich and powerful.[5] At the same time, the new disposability discourse expunges any sense of responsibility from both the body politic and the ever-expanding armies of well-paid anti-public intellectuals and politicians who fill the air waves with poisonous lies, stupidity, and ignorance, all in the name of so-called "common sense" and a pathological notion of freedom stripped of any concern for the lives and misfortunes of others. In the age of disposability, the dream of getting ahead has been replaced with, for many people, the struggle simply to stay alive. The logic of disposability and mean-spirited cruelty that now come out of the mouths of zombie-like politicians are more fitting for the authoritarian regimes that emerged in Russia and Germany in the 1930s rather than for any society that calls itself a democracy. A politics of uncertainty, insecurity, deregulation, and fear now circulates throughout the country as those marginalized by class and color become bearers of unwanted memories and are subjected to state-sanctioned acts of violence and rough justice. Poor minority youth, immigrants, and other disposable populations now become the flashpoint that collapses moral and political taxonomies in the face of a growing punishing state. Instead of becoming the last option, violence and punishment have become the standard response to confronting the problems of the poor, disadvantaged, and jobless. As Judith Butler points out, those considered "other" and disposable are viewed as "neither alive nor dead, but interminable spectral—human beings no longer regarded as human" (Butler 2004: 33).

Thinking about visions of the good society is now considered a waste of time. As Zygmunt Bauman points out, too many young people and adults

> are now pushed and pulled to seek and find individual solutions to socially created problems and implement those solutions individually using individual skills

---

5 For an excellent article on the politics of austerity and the need to apply such measures to the rich rather than the middle and working classes, see Wolff (2010).

and resources. This ideology proclaims the futility (indeed, counterproductivity) of solidarity: of joining forces and subordinating individual actions to a "common cause." It derides the principle of communal responsibility for the well-being of its members, decrying it as a recipe for a debilitating "nanny state," and warning against care for the other leading to an abhorrent and detestable "dependency."

(Bauman 2008: 88–89)

Tea Party candidates express anger over government programs, but say nothing about a government that provides tax breaks for the rich, allows politicians to be bought off by powerful lobbyists, contracts out government functions to private industries, and guts almost every major public sphere necessary for sustaining an increasingly faltering democracy. Tea Party members are outraged, but their anger is really directed at the New Deal, the social state, and all those others whom they believe do not qualify as "real" Americans.[6] At the same time, the American public is awash in a craven and vacuous media machine that routinely tells us that people are angry, but offers no analysis capable of treating such anger as symptomatic of an economic system that creates massive inequalities, rewards the ultra rich and powerful, and punishes everybody else.

Bob Herbert has recently argued that the rich and powerful are indifferent to poor people and, of course, he is right, but only partly so (Herbert 2010: A31). In actuality, it is much worse. Today's young people and others caught in webs of poverty and despair face not only the indifference of the rich and powerful but also the scorn of the very people charged with preserving, protecting, and defending their rights. We now live in a country in which the government allows entire populations and groups to be perceived and treated as disposable, reduced to fodder for the neoliberal waste management industries created by a market-driven society in which gross inequalities and massive human suffering are its most obvious by-products.[7] The anger among the American people is more than justified by the suffering many people are now experiencing, but an understanding of such anger is stifled largely by right-wing organizations and rich corporate zombies who want to preserve the nefarious conditions that produced such anger in the first place. The result is an egregious politics of disconnection, not to mention a fraudulent campaign of lies and innuendos funded by shadowy ultra-right billionaires such as the Koch brothers (Mayer 2010), the loss of historical memory amply supported in dominant media such as Fox News, and a massively funded, depoliticizing culture, all of which help to pave the way for the new barbarism and its increasing registers of cruelty, inequality, punishment, and **authoritarianism**.

---

6 I think E. J. Dionne, Jr., gets it right in his analysis of how marginal the Tea Party is to American politics. See Dionne (2010), p. A27. See also the important book by Will Bunch (2010).

7 See, for instance, Schwalbe (2008) and Wilkinson and Pickett (2010).

This is a politics that dare not speak its name—a politics wedded to inequity, exclusion, and disposability—beholden to what Richard Hofstadter once called the "paranoid style in American politics" (Hofstadter 1964). Driven largely by a handful of right-wing billionaires such as Rupert Murdoch, David and Charles Koch, and Sal Russo, this is a stealth politics masquerading as a grass-roots movement. Determined to maintain corporate power and the benefits it accrues for the few as a result of a vast network of political, social, and economic inequalities, this is a politics wedded to an irrational mode of capitalism that undermines any vestige of democracy. At the heart of the new politics of savagery is the drive for unchecked amounts of power and profits in spite of the fact that this brand of take-no-prisoners politics is largely responsible for both the economic recession and producing a society that is increasingly becoming politically dysfunctional and ethically unhinged. It is a fringe politics whose funding sources hide in the shadows, careful not to disclose the identities of the right-wing billionaire fanatics eager to finance ultra-conservative groups such as the Tea Party movement. While some Republicans seem embarrassed by the fact that the likes of Glenn Beck, Michele Bachmann, Rush Limbaugh, and Sarah Palin have taken over their party, most of its members still seem willing to embrace wholeheartedly the politics of inequality, exclusion, and disposability that lies at the heart of an organized death march aimed at destroying every public sphere essential to a vibrant democratic state.

The United States has not just lost its moral compass in a sea of collective anger, as some liberals seem to believe (given its history, the very notion of a moral compass is more of an ideal than a reality). Instead, it has become a country that is no longer able to connect reason and freedom, recognize the anti-democratic forces that now threaten it from within, and bolster its capacity to protect its citizens from the ravages of unscrupulous neoliberalism as it spreads like a plague across the globe. The spectacle of moral panics over immigrants, the wild fire of religious and racial bigotry, conscienceless support for unchecked inequality and corporate power, the endless reproduction of celebrity and consumer culture, and growing registers of shared fears now define American politics. The future is increasingly being shaped by barbarians who thrive on ignorance and stupidity, while reaping the rewards of big corporate power and money. Freedom is now tied to the making of instant fortunes largely by the corporate elite and to an individualistic ethic that disdains any notion of solidarity and social responsibility. The social state has become a garrison state committed to dismantling collective forms of insurance that cover individuals who suffer from debilitating and life-changing calamities, while simultaneously expanding the prison system and other elements of the human waste disposal industry.

What does it mean when a country denies basic social provisions to the young, poor, elderly, and those suffering from tragedies and hardships that are not of their own making and which cannot be addressed through the call to individual responsibility? What happens when the war on poverty becomes the war on the poor? What does it mean when the political state cedes its power to corporate power? Where is America going when it turns its back on its own children, condemning them to a life of poverty, hopelessness, and immeasurable suffering? What happens to a country when over 50 million people live in poverty, 1 in 5 youth lives below the poverty line, and a majority of politicians believes it is better to extend tax cuts for the ultra rich rather than invest in jobs, education, health care, and the future? In part, it means that youth are no longer viewed as a social investment or as a marker of adult social responsibility. Instead, young people today become an excess burden and are handed over to the marketing experts and the advocates of privatization and **commodification**. They attend schools that treat them like robots or criminals, while the most creative and brilliant teachers are deskilled, reduced to either technicians or cheerleaders for the billionaires' educational reform efforts. Young people are no longer a group to be nurtured, but a new market waiting to be mined for profits or an army used to fight immoral wars. When deemed necessary, these objectified youth are locked away from the glitter of the shopping malls and the scrubbed and gated middle- and ruling-class communities that float above the dark cesspools of inequality the privileged classes helped to create.

The working-class neighborhood of my youth never gave up on democracy as an ideal, in spite of how much it might have failed us. As an ideal, it offered the promise of a better future; it mobilized us to organize collectively in order to fight against injustice; and it cast an intense light on those who traded in corruption, unbridled power, and greed. Politics was laid bare in a community that expected more of itself and its citizens as it tapped into the promise of a democratic society. But like many individuals and groups today, democracy is now also viewed as disposable, considered redundant—a dangerous remnant of another age. And yet, like the memories of my youth, there is something to be found in those allegedly outdated ideals that may provide the only hope we have left for recognizing the anti-democratic politics, power relations, and reactionary ideologies espoused by the new barbarians.

Democracy as both an ideal and a reality is now under siege in a militarized culture of fear and forgetting. The importance of moral witnessing has been replaced by a culture of instant gratification and unmediated anger, just as forgetting has become an active rather than passive process; what the philosopher Slavoj Žižek calls a kind of "fetishist disavowal: 'I know, but I don't want to know that I know, so I don't know'" (2008: 53). The lights are going out in America. And the threat comes not from alleged irresponsible government spending, a growing deficit, or the specter of a renewed democratic social state. On the contrary, it comes from the dark forces of an economic Darwinism and its newly energized armies of right-wing financial sharks, shout-till-you-drop mobs, reactionary ideologues, powerful right-wing media conglomerates, and corporate-sponsored politicians who sincerely hope, if not yet entirely believe, that the age of democratization has come to an end and the time for a new and cruel politics of disposability and human waste management is at hand.

We are living through a period in American history in which politics has been commodified and depoliticized at the same moment as the civic courage of intellectuals, students, labor unions, and working people has receded from the public realm. Maybe it is time to reclaim a history not too far removed from my own youthful memories of when democracy as an ideal was worth struggling over; when public goods were more important than consumer durables; when the common good outweighed private privileges; and when the critical notion that a society can never be just enough was the real measure of civic identity and political health. Maybe it is time to reclaim the spirit of a diverse and powerful social movement willing to organize, speak out, educate, and fight for the promise of a democracy that would do justice to the dreams of a generation of young people waiting for adults to prove the courage of their democratic convictions. Hopefully, the young people now marching against corporate greed, power, and fraud in Zuccotti Park, Oakland, and across the globe will put a stop to the anti-democratic pressures and tendencies that are undermining their hopes for a more secure and democratic future. Clearly, any notion of a future different from the one they have been given is now almost exclusively in their hands.

III: Racialized Memories and Class Identities

Thinking about Youth in Post-9/11 America

❧━✕━❧

As a young kid growing up in Providence, Rhode Island, I was always conscious of what it meant to be a white male. Whiteness was a defining principle shaping how I both named and negotiated the class and racial boundaries along which my friends and I traveled when we went to school, played basketball in gyms throughout the city, and crossed into "alien" neighborhoods. Whiteness and maleness were crucial markers of our individual and collective identities. Yet we were also working class, and it was largely the interface of race and class that governed how we experienced and perceived the world around us. Of course, we hadn't thought deeply about race and class in a critical way—we simply bore the burdens, terrors, and advantages such terms provided as they simultaneously named the world and produced it. We were immersed in a culture infused with the markings of a racialized and class-based society, but had no language either to name it or to reflect on it in a serious way. We simply accepted the notion that such divisions were part of human nature, something we had to both live with and negotiate in the limited terms given to us by the dominant society.

In my white working-class neighborhood, race and class were **performative categories** defined in terms of the events, actions, and outcomes of our struggles as we engaged with kids whose histories, languages, and racial identities appeared foreign and hostile to us. Race and class were not merely nouns we used to narrate ourselves. They were verbs that governed how we interacted and performed in the midst of "others," whether they were white middle-class or black youths. Most of the interactions we had with others were violent, fraught with anger and hatred. We viewed kids who were black or privileged from within the spaces and enclaves of a neighborhood ethos that was nourished by a legacy of racism, a dominant culture that condoned class and racial hatred, and a popular culture that rarely allowed blacks and whites to view each other as equals, except, of course, in athletics. Everywhere we looked, segregation was the order of the day. Community was defined within racial and class differences and functioned largely as a space of exclusion, more often than not pitting racial and ethnic groups against one another. Solidarity was mostly based on establishing our differences from others, and race and class identities closed down the promise of diversity as central to any notion of democratic community.

When Providence College students walked through my Smith Hill neighborhood to reach the downtown section of the city, we taunted them, fought with them on occasion, but always made it clear to them that their presence violated our territorial and class boundaries. We viewed these kids as rich, spoiled, privileged, and different from us—and as a reminder of how little we counted in a society that seemed more concerned about punishing us than providing us with the resources that spoke to a more humane future. We hated their alleged arrogance and despised their Pat Boone-type music. Generally, we had no contact with middle-class kids until we went to high school. Hope High School (ironically named) in the 1960s was a mix of mostly poor black and white kids, on the one hand, and a small group of wealthy kids on the other. School authorities and administrators did everything they could to make sure that the only space we shared was the cafeteria during lunch hour. Generally, black and working-class white kids were warehoused and segregated in that school. Because we were tracked into dead-end courses, school became a form of dead time for most of us—a place in which our bodies, thoughts, and emotions were regulated and sub-jected to either ridicule or swift disciplinary action if we broke any of the rules. We moved within these spaces of hierarchy and segregation deeply resentful of how we were treated, but with little understanding and no vocabulary that would enable us to connect our personal rage to either larger social structures or viable forms of political resistance. We were trapped in a legacy of commonsensical and privatized understand-ings that made us complicitous with our own oppression. In the face of injustice, we learned to be aggressive and destructive, but we learned little about what it might mean to unlearn our prejudices and join in alliances with those diverse others who were oppressed in different, and sometimes similar, ways.

The everyday practices that shaped our lives were often organized around rituals of harsh discipline, rigid regulation, and ongoing acts of humiliation. While race was a more complicated register of discrimination, class registered its difference through a range of segregated spaces. For instance, the working-class black and white kids from my section of town entered Hope High School through the back door of the building, while the rich white kids entered through the main door in the front of the school. We didn't miss the point, and we did everything we could to let the teachers know how we felt about it. We were loud and unruly in classes; we shook the rich kids down and took their money after school; we cheated whenever possible; but more than anything, we stayed away from school until we were threatened with being expelled.

Along with the black kids in the school, our bodies rather than our minds were taken up as a privileged form of cultural capital. With few exceptions, the teachers and school administrators let us know that we were not bright enough to be in col-lege credit courses, but we were perhaps talented enough to be star athletes or do well in classes that stressed manual labor. Both working-class whites and blacks resented those students who studied, used middle-class language, and appeared to live outside of their physicality. We fought, desired, moved, and pushed our bodies to extremes, especially in those few public spheres open to us. For me, as a white youth, that meant the race track, the basketball court, and the baseball diamond.

As a working-class white kid, I found myself in classes with black kids, played basketball with them, and loved black music. But we rarely socialized outside of school. Whiteness in my neighborhood was a signifier of pride, a marker of racial identity experienced through a dislike of blacks. Identities were viewed as fixed, unchanging, and linked to complex notions of privilege. Unlike the current generation of working-class kids, we defined ourselves in opposition to blacks. While we listened to their music, we did not appropriate their styles. Racism ran deep in that neighborhood, and no one was left untouched by it. But identities are always in transit: they mutate, change, and often become more complicated as a result of chance encounters, traumatic events, or unexpected collisions.

The foundation of my white racist identity was shaken while I was in the ninth grade in the last year of junior high school. I was on the junior high basketball team along with a number of other white and black kids. The coach had received some tickets to a Providence College game. Providence College's basketball team had begun to receive extensive public attention because it had won a National Invitation Basketball tournament. The team roster also included a number of famous players such as Lenny Wilkens and Johnny Egan. We loved the way in which these guys played, and we tried to incorporate their every move into our own playing styles. Getting tickets to see them play was like a dream come true for us. Having only two tickets to give away, the coach held a contest after school in the gym to decide who would go to the game. He decided to give the tickets to the two players who made the most consecutive foul shots. The air was tense as we started to compete for the tickets. I ended up with two other players in a three-way tie and we had one chance to break it. As I approached the foul line, Brother Hardy, a large black kid, started taunting me as I began to shoot. We exchanged some insults, and suddenly we were on each other, fists flying. Within no time, I was on the floor, blood gushing out of my nose. The fight was over as quickly as it started. The coach made us continue the contest, and, ironically, Brother Hardy and I won the tickets, shook hands, and went to the game together. The fight bridged us together in a kind of mutual esteem we didn't quite understand, but respected. Soon afterward, we started hanging out together and became friends. After graduating from junior high school, we parted, and I didn't see him again until the following September when I discovered that he was also attending Hope High School.

I made the varsity team my sophomore year. Brother Hardy never bothered to try out. I never knew why. We talked once in a while in the school halls, but the racial boundaries in the school did not allow us to socialize much with each other. Our friendship had a lasting impact, however. The second month into the school year, I noticed that every day during lunch hour a number of black kids would cut in front of the white kids in the food line, shake them down, and take their lunch money. I was waiting for it to happen to me, but it never did. In fact, the same black kids who did the shaking down would often greet me with a nod, or say, "Hey, man, how you doin'?" as they walked by me in the corridors. I later learned that Brother Hardy was considered the toughest black kid in the school, and he had put out the word to his friends to leave me alone.

During the week, I played basketball at night at the Benefit Street Club, situated in the black section of the city. I was one of the few whites allowed to play in the gym. The games were fast and furious, and you had to be good to continue. I started hanging out with Brother Hardy again, and on the weekends went to the blues clubs with him and his friends. We drank, played basketball, and rarely talked to each other about race. Soon, some of my friends and I were crossing a racial boundary by attending parties with our black teammates. Few people in our old neighborhood knew that we had broken a racial taboo, and we refrained from telling them.

I couldn't articulate it in those formative years, but as I moved within and across a number of racially defined spheres, it slowly became clear to me that I had to reconsider how I understood my own whiteness and the racism that largely informed it. I had no intention of becoming a black wannabe, even if such an option had existed in the neighborhood in which I grew up, and of course it didn't. But at the same time, I began to hate the racism that shaped the identities of my white friends. My crossing of the racial divide was met at best with disdain, and at worst with ridicule. Crossing this border was never an option for Brother Hardy and his friends. If they had crossed the racial border to come into my neighborhood, they would have been met with racist epithets and violence. Even in the early sixties, it became clear to me that such border crossings were restricted and only took place with a passport stamped with the legacy of racial privilege. Yet, my body and its movements posed a challenge to the lessons of race and identity, and I was beginning to unlearn the racist ideologies that I had taken for granted for so long. But I still had no language to question critically how I felt, nor did I understand how exactly to interrogate and reject the notion that to be a working-class white kid meant one had to be a racist by default.

The language I inherited as a kid came from my family, friends, school, and the larger popular culture. Rarely did I encounter a vocabulary in any of these spheres that ruptured or challenged the material relations of racism or the stereotypes and prejudices that reinforced race and class divisions. It was only later, as the sixties unfolded, that I discovered in the midst of the civil rights and anti-war movement the languages of dissent and possibility that helped me to rethink my own memories of youth, masculinity, racism, and class discrimination.

In many ways, much of the scholarship I have undertaken in the past 30 years has been an attempt to engage in a form of **memory-work**—exploring how I was positioned and how I located myself within a range of discourses and institutional practices—in which it has become clear that racial and class differences fueled by bigotry, intolerance, and systemic inequality were disruptive and significant forces in my life. My own sense of what it meant to be a white male emerged performatively through my interactions with peers, the media, and the broader culture. The identifications I developed, the emotional investments I made, and the ideologies I used to negotiate my youth were the outcome of educational practices that appeared either to ignore or denigrate working-class people, women, and minority groups.

Popular culture provided the medium through which we learned how to negotiate our everyday lives, especially when it brought together elements of resistance found in Hollywood youth films such as *Blackboard Jungle* (1955) or the rock 'n' roll music of Bill Haley and the Comets, Elvis Presley, Fats Domino, Little Richard, Etta James, and other artists. Moreover, working-class street culture provided its own set of unique events and tensions in which our bodies, identities, and desires were both mobilized and constrained. We were the first generation of working-class kids for whom popular media such as television played a central role in not only legitimating our social roles but also limiting the range of possibilities through which we could imagine something beyond the world in which we lived. The trauma I associated with negotiating between the solidarity I felt with Brother Hardy and the racism of my white working-class friends suggested that education works best when those experiences that shape and penetrate one's lived reality are jolted, unsettled, and made the object of critical analysis.

In looking back on my experience of moving through the contested terrains of race, gender, and class, it became clear to me that power is never exerted only through economic control, but also through what might be called a form of **cultural pedagogy**. This is education at the hands of what C. Wright Mills called the **cultural apparatus**—an apparatus invested in, according to Pierre Bourdieu, distinguishing certain types of cultural capital as symbolic power and privilege. More specifically, cultural pedagogy refers to an array of different sites of mass and image-based media that have become a new and powerful pedagogical force, reconfiguring the very nature of politics, cultural production, engagement, and resistance. Racism and class hatred are learned activities, and as a kid I found myself in a society that was all too ready to teach them. Autobiography only takes us so far, but when our experiences are connected to history, it offers an important narrative for linking the personal to the political, while also enabling us to translate private issues into public considerations. And it is these personal memories of my own experience with the indignities and power structures of race and class that bear so heavily on how I now mediate those forces at a much different period in my life.

Today, I find the racism that shaped my youth has resurfaced with a vengeance, and yet seems to be abstracted from any sense of the past, particularly the civil rights struggles that fought for racial justice. The emergence of a new racist cultural pedagogy became apparent, if not celebrated, with the infamous Willie Horton political ad run by George H. W. Bush during the 1988 presidential campaign. The Willie

Horton ad was particularly offensive for its overt racism. The ad first makes a pitch for the death penalty and then points out that Willie Horton (whose actual name was William), a black man who was in prison as the result of a murder conviction, was released 10 times under a furlough program during Gov. Dukakis's term. During one of those releases, he kidnapped a young couple, and proceeded to stab the boy and rape the young girl. The ad concludes with the comment, "Weekend prison passes. Dukakis on crime." While there were many more white people than black involved in this program, the ad focused on the image of a black man. The racist message implied that Dukakis was not only soft on crime, but that he was especially soft on black criminals and, as a liberal, supported a culture of criminality that was exclusively black and particularly dangerous to Bush's white, conservative, and suburban following.

Racism today has been reconfigured as "color blind" in terms of who it victimizes, and social and systemic forces have been rendered invisible by a growing discourse of privatization. In the first instance, racism now represents an attack on white people who see themselves as on the receiving end of a so-called "reverse racism" perpetrated by black power structures and black politicians. This is most obvious in the remarks of a number of infamous politicians and media celebrities. For example, Glenn Beck claimed on Fox News that President Obama was "a racist" who has "a deep-seated hatred for white people" and compared his administration to the "Planet of the Apes." Rush Limbaugh has called Obama a "halfrican American" and repeatedly played a song on his radio show unapologetically titled "Barack the Magic Negro." All the while the dominant media say little about how these comments are symptomatic of a vile racism that has gained increasing respectability since the 1980s. When the well-known talk radio host Dr. Laura Schlessinger went out of her way to use the N-word 11 times in 15 minutes in order to humiliate a black female caller, the press largely focused on the event as an expression of unfortunate and erratic behavior (for which Dr. Laura later apologized). In the face of Dr. Laura's decision to retire from her radio program, Sarah Palin used Twitter to fire off some advice to her: "don't retreat … reload." This blatant support for a racial slur coupled with a metaphor for violence does more than mimic the worst elements of the Jim Crow south. It points to how the legacy of racism is both forgotten and simultaneously updated to fuel a virulent new form of racialized fear and hatred. When the mainstream media discovered that Rick Perry, one of the Republicans running for the presidency in 2012, leased a hunting ranch which had a rock at the front of the camp inscribed with the offensive word "Niggerhead," only one member of the Republican Party criticized him for it, and that member was an African American.

It appears that much can be forgiven in a society where it is increasingly believed that white men are now under attack by black people or, for that matter, class warfare is something that positions the financial elite as victims. Racist paranoia can be seen in attacks against the image of a black president who is allegedly a Muslim in disguise. The troubling and insidious claim being made daily by right-wing politicians and others is that the public sphere exists primarily as the preserve of white Christians. This claim all too obviously equates white Christianity with a defense of American nationhood, citizenship, and patriotism. Unfortunately, such a monstrous claim is rarely challenged in the dominant media. Without an understanding of how culture constitutes and legitimates our reality, racism is reduced to a poor choice of words on the part of an individual, deemed perhaps to reflect unfortunate personal taste but to be pretty much harmless at the level of broader society. Hence, foul racist remarks are treated as bad jokes, indiscreet humor, or a harmless species of opinion. They are dissociated from even a hint of the structural racism and accompanying power relations that have become increasingly felt, while remaining largely invisible, in the United States. One obvious example of this strategy can be found in the way in which the current intense racism directed against Muslims, exemplified in numerous remarks made by conservative politicians and talk radio hosts, is viewed as simply an expression of anger rather than a species of virulent racism.

Echoes of racism now present themselves in multiple forms and are spreading across the country like a highly contagious virus. This is obvious in terms of a racist cultural pedagogy propagated largely through a right-wing cultural apparatus. But its traces and effects can also be found in acts of real violence that run like a highly charged electric current through the mainstream media, which reproduce representations of racist violence while failing to comment on them critically. Consequently, when right-wing journalists, bloggers, and politicians make comments about Obama instituting socialism, death panels, concentration camps, and mass round-ups, such comments are dealt with simply as either individual opinions or individual prejudices. Individual free speech now trumps any claim to social and racial justice. At the same time, state and structural racism are no longer viewed as significant forces in shaping contemporary American society, which is now safely ensconced in a market-driven discourse that imagines itself free of racism, a belief apparently legitimated by the election of the first African-American president. Not surprisingly in this alleged era of a post-civil rights society, politics has become more racialized even as the discourse about race has become more privatized, reduced to the realm of psychology, emotive disorders, individual responsibility, or that old line of defense, free speech.

Any talk about the political and material transformation of a deeply racial social order is largely off the radar for the mainstream media, if not for most of the American public. Consequently, it comes as no surprise that the dominant media have largely refused to connect the racism characteristic of the current debates—the resistance to building a mosque near Ground Zero, for example—to a more comprehensive political and cultural agenda or even to the escalating and brutal burnings of mosques and violence being waged against Muslims in other parts of the United States. The barely disguised racism at work in this controversy is simply treated as another opinion, an expression of post-9/11 anger, legitimated by the principle of free speech. What is disturbing about these words and actions is how they both register an alarming growth of racism in the United States and indicate how the escalating of racist name calling and the proliferation of racist representations easily move into a nightmarish siege mentality brimming with the threat, if not actual practice, of violence. As insecurities and anxieties grow among the American public in the midst of an economic recession, state and federal governments fail to offer substantive reforms. Racial, religious, cultural, and class hatred become convenient vehicles for focusing the diffuse anger produced by untold hardship and suffering, thereby allowing right-wing corporate and religious drones to promote their ideological and political agendas while enhancing their celebrity status and raking in large profits.

Growing up in the fifties and sixties, I witnessed how egregious acts of racism—such as the killing and torture of Emmett Till, the beatings of civil rights demonstrators, and the humiliation suffered by Rosa Parks—sparked major demonstrations, mobilizations, and social movements dedicated to fighting racism. Racism was brutally exercised, but did not escape the scrutiny and public shame the country rightly felt about it. Today, there is no shame attached to racism because it is no longer viewed as a social problem, but merely an individual issue. When its poisonous rhetoric and policies emerge, we seem to lack any vocabulary or historical awareness for addressing it, except through the discourse of those fanning the flames of racial injustice.

How else to explain the willingness of many Americans to accept Glenn Beck's claim that he is appropriating the language of the civil rights movement while at the same time spewing out daily the most offensive racial commentaries? What are we to make of NBC's Brian Williams revisiting New Orleans on a heavily promoted *Dateline* special, "Hurricane Katrina: The First Five Days," and focusing in a self-congratulatory manner on how well the media covered the event? Lost in his analysis was any commentary on the racist policies that defined the Bush administration's response to Katrina or the racist brutality exercised in the aftermath of the storm by elements of the New Orleans Police Department. Instead, he reinforced the myths that Katrina was a natural tragedy, rather than a political one, and that violence was out of control in the days following the tragedy—a misconstruction that has been exposed as false by none other than the New Orleans *Times-Picayune*. The media in this instance did not merely fail to report adequately on the events and response leading up to Katrina but also became complicit in once again suggesting that African-American culture is largely a culture of violence. Clearly, we need to pay attention to how race is being spoken about in our dominant media and everyday language, just as we need to examine the cultural and social formations that benefit from class and racial injustices. We need to remind ourselves about how race and class injustices undermine the fabric of democracy.

As a child growing up in the midst of racial segregation, I witnessed instances when the gap between America's democratic ideals and the reality of class inequality and racial injustice was made visible. At the same time, there were spaces and movements of resistance, and a trace of democratic idealism, running through the sixties and President Lyndon Johnson's image of the "Great Society." While such idealism often covered over a host of injustices, it did provide a political and ethical referent for thinking about and acting on the difference between the existing state of things and the promise of a substantive democratic polity. I think that any lingering idealism of this kind has turned to cynicism in America. The gap between the rich and the poor, the powerful and the powerless, has grown larger than ever. Deepening inequalities along with the misery and human suffering these gaps produce are out of control. Moreover, everywhere we turn, the shadow of Jim Crow is engulfing the policies, practices, and discourses about race in America. The racial segregation of public schooling is greater today than in the sixties; racism is on full display in the increasing collective anger waged against Muslims; the prison has become the pre-eminent public space for black youth; and poor minorities of class and color, faced with the racialized burdens of poverty and unemployment, are now viewed by politicians, the dominant media, and the general public as largely disposable, a drain on the public coffers and unworthy of social protections. The emergence of a neoliberal market-based order is a driving force behind this new era of racial inequality and violence. Confronted with such a dangerous moment in the proliferation of multiple forms of racism, America appears to have lost its capacity to bear witness, as the avatars of racism are now treated in the dominant media as reflecting just another ideological position or, even worse, just one opinion among many.

The pathology of racism and the growing inequality impacting those marginalized by race, class, gender, and age suggest the emergence of a society in which we no longer believe in the humanity of the other. Instead, too many Americans seem to believe and support the notion that humanity has lost its claim on democracy, and democracy is no longer worth fighting for. The deeper causes of class inequality and racial injustice have been drowned out by the shouting and demagoguery of a group of radical authoritarians who control the cultural apparatuses in America and make any form of legitimate politics dysfunctional. They speak of a new American dream and civil rights movement, but they lack either the imagination or the ethics to be taken seriously, especially given how much they despise democracy, thrive on racist and class-based social relations, and disdain any vestige of the social state.

If we are going to take democracy seriously, it is time for social movements, parents, unions, intellectuals, and alternative media to address individually and collectively the growing racism and class inequality head on as part of a new post-civil rights struggle.[1] This means fighting for public services, emboldening the social state, waging a cultural war in which progressive opinions and democratic values can be heard, and connecting various independent struggles as part of one larger movement for radical democracy. Central to such a struggle is the battle over ideas and power. Struc-

---

1 On this issue, see Searls Giroux (2010).

tures of power—whether they be in the realm of economics, politics, or culture—will not change by themselves. The struggle for ideas, subjectivities, desires, and different modes of agency requires that pedagogy and education, along with the public spheres that make them possible, become a primary concern for any form of politics that believes in the principles of reason and freedom. We are at a watershed in American history, and dark clouds are forming on the horizon. The price to be paid for living in this increasingly privatized, consumer-oriented, and corporate-dominated culture is almost too bleak to imagine. But we have to both imagine it and then organize in every way possible to prevent it. Maybe it is time to stop the wars abroad and focus on a new battle that takes seriously those anti-democratic forces ready to plunge America into the grip of authoritarianism.

IV: Beyond America's Culture of Cruelty

The term 'cruelty' is chosen by convention to indicate those forms of extreme violence, whether intentional or systemic, physical or moral … that seem to be, as is said 'worse than death' … the actual or virtual menace of cruelty represents for politics, and particularly for politics today … a crucial experiment in which the very possibility of politics is at stake.

Etienne Balibar (2004: 6)

Under the current regime of market-driven economic Darwinism, a **culture of cruelty** and **politics of humiliation** have gained momentum in American society. Cruelty and humiliation appear to have become both commonplace and no longer in need of legitimation. They have become normalized, accepted largely as a matter of common sense. The tragic violence and mass killing committed by Jared Lee Loughner in Tucson, Arizona in 2011 cannot be reduced to the mental instability of a young man out of touch with reality. Nor can such a horrendous act be reduced to a breakdown in civil discourse or the increasing absence of any viable gun control regulations. Mental health, a wild-west gun culture, and the lack of civility in politics, especially in the age of hate talk radio and the call to violence that underpins the discourses of the likes of Sarah Palin, Michele Bachmann, and other right-wing politicians, are significant issues. The growing public enthusiasm for violent speech, a media saturated with spectacles of violence, and the growing lawlessness of Wall Street bankers and high finance are matched by "a growing faith in force as the solution to almost any problem, whether at home or abroad" (Schell 2011). Yet, such rationales are too easy, and emulate what might be called a classic case of American denial. There is a deeper order of politics behind this murderous act, one that the American public is inclined to ignore. More specifically, the general responses to this violent act are symptomatic of a society that separates private injuries from public considerations and, in doing so, refuses to connect individual acts to broader social considerations. Violence is no longer understood as an important measure of the need for a society to reform itself. It has been depoliticized, reduced to either entertainment, a source of instant pleasure, or relegated to the province of an individual pathology.

I want to suggest that underlying the Arizona shootings is a culture of cruelty that has become so widespread in American society that the violence it produces is largely taken for granted, often dismissed in terms that cut it off from any larger systemic forces at work in the society, such as militarism, the rise of the security state, the war economy, the ever-expanding machinery of empire. The culture of cruelty is important for thinking through how entertainment and politics now converge in ways that fundamentally transform how we understand and imagine politics in the current historical moment—a moment when the central issue of getting by is no longer about working to get ahead but struggling simply to survive. And many groups who are considered marginal because they are poor, unemployed, people of color, elderly, or young have not just been excluded from "the American dream," but have become utterly redundant and disposable, waste products of a society that no longer considers them of any value. How else to explain the zealousness with which social safety nets have been dismantled, the transition from welfare to workfare (offering few job training programs and no childcare), and recent acrimony over health care reform's public option? What accounts for the passage of laws that criminalize the behavior of the 1.2 million homeless in the United States, often defining sleeping, sitting, soliciting, lying down, or loitering in public places as a criminal offense rather than a behavior that should elicit compassionate good will and public assistance? Where is the outrage over a war on drugs that resembles the worst offenses of slavery? For example, as Michelle Alexander has pointed out, "there are more African-American men under the control of the criminal justice system than were enslaved in 1850 and because of the war on drugs four out of five black youth in some communities can expect to be either in prison or caught up in the criminal justice system at some point in their lives."[1] Or, for that matter, the expulsions, suspensions, segregation, class discrimination, and racism in the public schools as well as the severe beatings, broken bones, and damaged lives endured by young people in the juvenile justice system?

Growing within the social structure is a hidden dimension of cruelty, one in which the powers of life and death are increasingly determined by punishing apparatuses, such as a racist criminal justice system for people of color or ruthless market forces for the poor. A competitive and punishing mentality increasingly infiltrates politics and public institutions and, in doing so, garners the authority to dictate who may live and who may die. A crucial element supporting these changes in governance and public sentiment is the growing cultural dominance of a right-wing media forged in pedagogy of hate that provides numerous platforms for a culture of cruelty. This form of cultural pedagogy is increasingly characterized by more than a breach of civility. It legitimates and registers without apology hostility towards immigrants, a barely disguised racism, contempt for the poor, and disdain for anyone who supports the social contract and the welfare state. Citizenship is increasingly constructed through an ideology of hyper-individualism and a language of contempt for all non-commercial

---

1 Cited in Price (2011). See also Alexander (2010).

public spheres. A chilling indifference to the plight of others is increasingly expressed in vicious tirades against "big government" and health care reform. All this signals a growing scorn on the part of the American public for any human beings caught in the web of misfortune, human suffering, dependency, and deprivation.

When I refer to a **culture of cruelty** and a discourse of humiliation, I am talking about the institutionalization and widespread adoption of a set of values, policies, and symbolic practices that legitimate forms of organized violence against human beings increasingly considered disposable, leading inexorably to unnecessary hardship, suffering, and despair. Such practices are increasingly accompanied by forms of humiliation in which the character, dignity, and bodies of targeted individuals and groups are under attack. Its extreme form is evident in state-sanctioned torture practices, such as those used by the regime of torture promoted by the Bush administration in Iraq and in the images of humiliation that emerged from the torture chambers of Abu Ghraib prison. The **politics of humiliation** is central to new modes of authoritarianism that work through various cultural apparatuses, diverse modes of address, and varied framing mechanisms in which the targeted subjects are represented in terms that demonize them, strip them of their humanity, and position them in ways that invite ridicule and sometimes violence. This is what the late Pierre Bourdieu called the symbolic dimension of power—that is, the capacity of systems of meaning, signification, and diverse modes of communication to shield, strengthen, and normalize relations of domination through distortion, misrepresentation, and the use of totalizing narratives (Wacquant 2005: 134). The hidden order of such politics lies not just in its absences, but in its appeal to common sense and its claim to being objective and apolitical. Culture in this sense becomes the site of the most powerful and persuasive forms of pedagogy precisely because it gets away with denying its pedagogical function.

Such practices and the cultural politics that legitimize them are apparent in zero-tolerance policies in schools, which mindlessly punish poor whites and students of color by criminalizing behavior as trivial as violating a dress code. Such students have been assaulted by the police, handcuffed, taken away in police cars, and in some cases imprisoned (Giroux 2009a). The discourse of humiliation, as mentioned above, also abounds in the public sphere of hate radio and Fox News, which provide a forum for pundits who trade in insults against feminists, environmentalists, African Americans, immigrants, progressive critics, liberal media, President Barack Obama, and anyone else who rejects the militant orthodox views of the new media extremists and religious fundamentalists. Policies that humiliate and punish are visible in the increasing expansion of the criminal justice system, used regularly to deal with problems that would be better addressed through social reforms than punishment. Homeless people are now arrested for staying too long in public libraries, sleeping in public parks, and soliciting money on the streets of many urban centers. People who receive welfare benefits are increasingly harassed by government agencies. Debtors' prisons are making a comeback as millions of people are left with no recourse but to default on the myriad of bills they cannot pay.[2] The growing numbers of people who are jobless, homeless, and increasingly living beneath the poverty line are treated by the government and dominant media as mere statistical fodder for determining the health of the GNP, while their lived experience of hardship is rarely mentioned. Millions of people are denied health care, regardless of how ill they might be, because they cannot afford it. Rather than enact social protections such as adequate health care for everyone, the advocates of free-market fundamentalism enact social policies that leave millions of people uninsured and designated largely as disposable populations who should fend for themselves.

The growing culture of cruelty in the United States has become a pivotal educational machine, often commercializing, brutalizing, and infantilizing what it touches. It is evident in the widespread sanctioning of violence and disdain for human life, especially for the lives of those marginalized by race and class. A survival-of-the-fittest mentality is exhibited daily on reality TV shows and in video games, extreme sports, Hollywood films, shock radio, and a variety of other forms of screen culture. Instead of capitulating to the worst elements of economic Darwinism, we need a formative culture unfettered by the forces of consumerism, violence, and a theater of cruelty. At the same time, we need a democratized cultural apparatus that provides the public spheres and critical vocabularies for defining vital social institutions as a public good, embracing a meaningful spirituality, promoting empathy and compassion, and legitimating shared values rather than shared fears. The cultural politics of casino capitalism, with its corporate controlled media machine, has numbed our sense of social and moral responsibility. Against this moral coma, with its theater of cruelty and legalized irresponsibility, we need to recast the language of politics. We must create public spheres and pedagogical practices that celebrate the public good, public life, civic courage, compassion, and meaningful spirituality as central to overcoming the privatizing and depoliticizing language of the market and the moral vacuity of casino capitalism. Both pedagogy and the educational force of the cultural apparatus are crucial to any viable language of democratic politics.

If it is true that a new form of authoritarianism is developing in the United States, undercutting any vestige of a democratic society, then it is equally true that there is nothing inevitable about this growing threat.[3] The long and tightening grip of authoritarianism in American political culture can be resisted and transformed. This dystopic future will not happen if intellectuals, workers, young people, and diverse social movements unite to create the public spaces and unsettling formative educational cultures necessary for reimagining the meaning of radical democracy. In part, this is a pedagogical project, one that recognizes consciousness, agency, spirituality, and education

---

2 See Editorial, "The New Debtors' Prisons," *New York Times* (April 5, 2009), p. A24.

3 On the new modes of authoritarianism, see Wolin (2008); Giroux (2008); Hedges (2010); and Hacker and Pierson (2010).

as central to any viable notion of politics. It is also a project designed to address, critique, and make visible the commonsense ideologies that enable neoliberal capitalism and other elements of an emerging authoritarianism to function alongside a kind of moral coma and imposed forgetting at the level of everyday life.

Evidence of such a project is visible in the multidimensional political and pedagogical work being done at online magazines and news sources such as *Alternet*, *Tikkun*, and *Truthout*. It is also visible in the Freechild Project, which organizes youth groups to fight against the many injustices young people face in the United States. Another site for such a project is in the work of the Media Education Foundation, which provides films, movies, and interviews for a wider informed public audience. All of these organizations engage in cultural practices and forms of public pedagogy that make visible the exercise of ruthless power on a number of fronts. They engage in a form of memory-work and public outreach that create the conditions for individuals and groups to develop alternative public spheres in which dialogue and exchange combine with varied forms of political intervention.

A social movement based on these principles will gain momentum only if the American public begins to recognize how the mechanisms of authoritarianism and the culture of cruelty have impacted their lives, restructured negatively the notion of freedom, and corrupted power by placing it largely in the hands of ruling elites, corporations, and different segments of the military and national security state. Such a project must work to develop vigorous social spheres and communities that promote a culture of deliberation, public debate, and critical exchange across a wide variety of cultural and institutional sites in an effort to generate democratic movements for social change. At stake here is the construction of a politics bolstered by a formative culture that creates the ideological and structural conditions necessary for a broad-based social movement that can move beyond the legacy of a fractured left or progressive politics in order to address the totality of the society's problems. This suggests finding a common ground where challenging diverse forms of oppression, exploitation, and exclusion can become part of a broader challenge to create a radical democracy. We need to develop an educated and informed public that embraces a culture of questioning capable of interrogating society's commanding institutions. We live at a time that demands a vocabulary that offers both critique and possibility, one that recognizes that without an informed citizenry, collective struggle, and viable social movements, democracy will slip out of our reach, no longer recognizable or considered worth struggling for. Without people standing up and organizing against this impending disaster, we will arrive at a new stage of history marked by a culture of cruelty and authoritarian politics that not only disdain all vestiges of democracy but are more than willing to relegate it to a distant memory.

V: Youth Fighting Back in the Age of Casino Capitalism

⤛⤜

In the face of the massive protests by young people around the globe, many media pundits have raised questions about why comparable forms of widespread resistance are not taking place among American youth. Everyone from progressive academics to mainstream radio commentators has voiced surprise and disappointment that American youth appear uninspired by the collective action of their counterparts in other countries. In a wave of global protests that indicted the lack of vision, courage, and responsibility on the part of their elders and political leaders, young people in many parts of the globe have recently taken history into their own hands. Fighting not merely for a space to survive, but also for a society in which matters of justice, dignity, and freedom are objects of collective struggle, these demonstrations have signaled a new stage in which young people once again are defining what John Pilger calls the "theater of the possible" (Pilger 2011). Signaling a generational and political crisis that is global in scope, young people have sent a message to the world that they refuse to live any longer under repressive authoritarian regimes sustained by morally bankrupt market-driven policies and repressive governments. Throughout Europe, students are protesting the attack on the social state, the savagery of neoliberal policies, and the devaluation of higher education as a public good. In doing so, they have defied a social order in which they could not work at a decent job, have access to a quality education, or support a family—a social order that offered them only a life stripped of self-determination and dignity.

Some commentators, including Courtney Martin, a senior correspondent for *The American Prospect*, have suggested that the problem is one of privilege. In a 2010 article for that magazine titled "Why Class Matters in Campus Activism," Martin argues that American students are often privileged and view politics as something that happens elsewhere, far removed from local activism (Martin 2010). Student politics in such instances might focus on poverty in India or on the recent environmental disasters in Haiti and Japan; when political issues emerge closer to home, in their own country, it is often ignored by organized student movements. Martin suggests not only that privileged middle-class kids are somehow the appropriate vanguard of change for this generation, but that they suffer from both a narcissistic refusal to look inward and an ego-driven sense of politics that is as narrow as it is paternalistic and missionary

focus. This critique is too simple, lacks complexity, and appears to suffer from the
same problem to which it is objecting.

The other side of the over-privileged youth argument is suggested by long-time
activist Tom Hayden, who argues that many students are so saddled with financial
debt and focused on what it takes to get a job that they have little time for political
activism (ibid.). According to Hayden, student activism in the United States, especially since the 1980s, has been narrowly issues-based, ranging from a focus on student
unionization and gender equity to environmental issues and greater minority enroll-
ment, thus circumscribing in advance youth participation in larger political spheres
(Edelman Boren 2001: 227). While Martin and Hayden both offer enticing narratives
to explain the current lack of student resistance, Simon Talley, a writer for *Campus
Progress*, may be closer to the truth in claiming that students in the United States have
less of an investment in higher education than European students because for the last
30 years they have been told that higher education neither serves a public good nor is
an invaluable democratic public sphere (Talley 2010).

These commentators, however much they sometimes get it right, still underestimate
the historical and current impacts of the conservative political climate on American
campuses and the culture of youth protest, especially since the 1980s. This conserva-
tism took firm hold with the election of Ronald Reagan and the emergence of both
neoconservative and neoliberal disciplinary apparatuses since the 1980s. Youth have
in fact been very active in the last few decades, but in many instances for deeply conservative ends. As Susan Searls Giroux has argued, a series of well-funded, right-wing
campus organizations have made much use of old and new media to produce best-
selling screeds as well as interactive websites for students to report injustices in the
interests of protesting the alleged left-totalitarianism of the academy. "Conservative
think tanks provide $20 million annually to the campus Right" to fund campus orga-
nizations such as Young Americans for Freedom, the Intercollegiate Studies Institute,
Students for Academic Freedom, and the Leadership Institute "which trains, supports
and does public relations for 213 conservative student groups who are provided with
suggestions for inviting conservative speakers to campus, help starting conservative
newspapers, or training to win campus elections" (Searls Giroux 2010: 79).

Liberal students, for their part, have engaged in forms of activism that mimic
market-driven modes of behavior. The increasing emphasis on consumerism, immediate gratification, and the narcissistic ethic of privatization took its toll in a range of
student protests developed over issues such as the right to party and "a defense of the
right to consume alcohol." As Mark Edelman Boren points out in his informative
book on student resistance, alcohol-related issues caused student uprisings on a number of American campuses. In one telling example, he writes,

> At Ohio University, several thousand students rioted in April 1998 for a second
> annual violent protest over the loss of an hour of drinking when clocks were offi-

cially set back at the beginning of daylight savings time; forced out of area bars, upset students hurled rocks and bottles at police, who knew to show up in full riot gear after the previous year's riot. The troops finally resorted to shooting wooden "knee-knocker" bullets at the rioters to suppress them.

(Edelman Boren 2001: 228)

All of these explanations have some merit in their attempt to account for the lack of resistance among American students within the last few decades, but I would like to shift the focus of the conversation. Student resistance in the United States must, I argue, always be viewed within a broader political landscape that, with few exceptions, remains unexamined. In the first instance, we have to remember that students in Western Europe, in particular, are faced with a series of crises that are more immediate, bold, and radical in their assault on young people and the institutions that bear down heavily on their lives than those in the United States. In the face of the economic recession, educational budgets are being cut in take-no-prisoners extreme fashion; the social state is being radically dismantled; tuition costs have spiked exponentially; and unemployment rates for young people are far higher than in the United States (with the exception of American youth in poor minority communities). European students have experienced a massive and bold assault on their lives, educational opportunities, and futures. Moreover, European students live in societies where it becomes more difficult to collapse public life into largely private considerations. Students in these countries have access to a wider range of critical public spheres; politics in many of these countries has not collapsed entirely into the spectacle of celebrity/commodity culture; left-oriented political parties still exist; and labor unions have more political and ideological clout than they do in the United States. Alternative newspapers, progressive media, and a profound sense of the political constitute elements of a vibrant, critical formative culture within a wide range of public spheres that have helped nurture and sustain the possibility to think critically, engage in political dissent, organize collectively, and inhabit public spaces in which alternative and critical theories can be developed.

Because of the diverse nature of how higher education is financed and governed in the United States, the assault on colleges and universities has been less uniform and differentially spread out among community colleges, public universities, and elite colleges, thus lacking a unified, oppressive narrative against which to position resistance. Moreover, the campus "culture wars" narrative has served to galvanize many youth around a reactionary cultural project while distancing them from the very nature of the economic and political assault on their future. All this suggests that another set of questions has to be raised. The more important questions—ones that do not reproduce the all-too-commonplace demonization of young people as merely apathetic— are twofold. First, the issue should not be why there have been no student protests, but why have the protests that have happened not been more widespread, linked, and sustained? The student protests against the draconian right-wing policies attempting to destroy union rights and the collective bargaining power of teachers supported by Republican Governor Scott Walker in Wisconsin is one example indicating that students are in fact engaged and concerned. The growing Occupy Wall Street protest movement is another example of youth becoming more active in organizing and demonstrating against the right-wing economic Darwinism that is destroying their future. There are also smaller student protests taking place at various colleges, including Berkeley and CUNY, and on other campuses throughout the United States. But student activists appear to constitute a minority of American students, with very few of these enrolled in professional programs. Most student activists are coming from the arts, social sciences, and humanities (the conscience of the college). Second, there is the crucial issue regarding what sort of conditions young people have inherited in a society that has undermined their ability to be critical agents capable of waging a massive protest movement against the growing injustices they face on a daily basis. After all, the assault on higher education in the United States, while not as severe as in Europe, still provides ample reasons for students to be in the streets protesting. Close to 43 states have pledged major cuts to higher education in order to compensate for insufficient state funding. This means an unprecedented hike in tuition rates is being implemented; enrollments are being slashed; salaries are being reduced; and needs-based scholarships in some states are being eliminated. Pell Grants, which allow poor students to attend college, are also being cut.[1] Robert Reich has chronicled some of the impacts on university budgets, which include cutting state funding for higher education by $151 million in Georgia; reducing student financial aid by $135 million in Michigan; raising tuition by 15 percent in Florida's 11 public universities; and increasing tuition by 40 percent in just two years at the University of California (Reich 2010). Although these increases seem particularly striking, tuition has been steadily rising over the past several decades and has become a disturbingly normative feature of post-secondary education.

One reason students have not protested these cuts in large numbers, until more recently, may be that by the time the average American student now graduates, he or she has not only a degree but also an average debt of about $23,000.[2] As Jeffrey Williams points out, this debt amounts to a growing form of indentured servitude

---

1   The government provides some excellent material on tuition increases for every college in the nation, covering the period from August 2009 to 2010. The statistics are staggering and point to increases on the average of around 45 percent. See http://collegecost.ed.gov/index.aspx?ebe6b8e1ed eae8c4cbc0bfcea1efeddce9e

2   There are many books and articles that take up this issue. One of the most incisive commentators is Jeffrey Williams (2008).

for many students that undercuts any viable notion of social activism and is further exacerbated by the fact that "unemployment for recent college graduates rose from 5.8 percent to 8.7 percent in 2009" (Mascriotra 2010). Crippling debt plus few job opportunities in a society in which individuals are relentlessly held as solely responsible for the problems they experience leaves little room for rethinking the importance of larger social issues and the necessity for organized collective action against systemic injustice. In addition, as higher education increasingly becomes a fundamental requirement for employment, many universities have reconfigured their mission exclusively in corporate terms, replacing education with training, and defining students as consumers, faculty as a cheap form of subaltern labor, and "entire academic departments as revenue generating units" (Head 2011). No longer seen as a social or public good, higher education is increasingly viewed less as a site of struggle than as a credential mill for success in the global economy.

Meanwhile, not only have academic jobs been disappearing, but given the shift to a business-driven education that is decidedly technicist in nature, students have been confronted for quite some time with a vanishing culture for sustained critical thinking. As universities and colleges emphasize market-based skills, students are learning neither how to think critically nor how to connect their private troubles with larger public issues. The humanities continue to be downsized, eliminating some of the most important opportunities many students will ever have to develop a commitment to public values, social responsibilities, and the broader demands of **critical citizenship**. Moreover, critical thinking has been devalued as a result of the growing **corporatization of higher education**. Under the influence of corporate values, thought in its most operative sense loses its *modus operandi* as a critical meditation on "civilization, existence, and forms of evaluation" (Nancy 2010: 9). Increasingly, it has become difficult for students to recognize how their education in the broadest sense has been systematically devalued, and how this not only undercuts their ability to be engaged critics but contributes to the further erosion of what is left of U.S. democracy. How else to explain the reticence of students in protesting against tuition hikes? The forms of instrumental training they receive undermine any critical capacity to connect the fees they pay to the fact that the United States puts more money into the funding of war, armed forces, and military weaponry than the next 25 countries combined—money that could otherwise fund higher education.[3] The inability both to be critical of such injustices and to relate them to a broader understanding of politics suggests a failure to think outside of the conceptual limitations and sensibilities of a neoliberal ideology that isolates knowledge and normalizes its own power relations. In fact, one recent study by Richard Arum and Josipa Roksa found that "45 percent of students

---

3 See Engelhardt (2010). See also Bacevich (2005) and Johnson (2006).

show no significant improvement in the key measures of critical thinking, complex reasoning and writing by the end of their sophomore years."[4]

The **corporatization of schooling** over the last few decades has done more than make universities into adjuncts of corporate power. It has produced a culture of critical illiteracy and further undermined the conditions necessary to enable students to become truly engaged political agents. The value of knowledge is now linked to a crude instrumentalism, and the only mode of education that seems to matter is that which enthusiastically endorses learning marketable skills, embracing a survival-of-the-fittest ethic, and defining the good life solely through accumulation and disposal of the latest consumer goods. Academic knowledge has been stripped of its value as a social good. Under these conditions, to be relevant and therefore funded, knowledge has to justify itself in market terms, or simply perish.

Enforced privatization, the closing down of critical public spheres, the conservative pedagogical influence of a powerful cultural apparatus, and the endless commodification of all aspects of social life have created a generation of students who are increasingly being reared in a society that tells them that politics is irrelevant. Public pedagogy, or the expansive pedagogical practices that now take place through major cultural apparatuses such as mainstream electronic and print media and other elements of screen culture, is increasingly dominated by right-wing ideology, and the struggle for democracy is being erased from social memory. This is not to suggest that Americans have abandoned the notion that ideas have power or that ideologies can move people. It means, unfortunately, that the institutions and cultural apparatuses that generate such ideas seem to be primarily controlled by the corporate media, right-wing think tanks, and other conservative groups.

While progressives appear willing to challenge right-wing ideologies and policies, they are less inclined to acknowledge the diverse ways in which culture functions in the production, distribution, and regulation of power. Culture works both as a set of representations through which individuals look at the world and as a pedagogical force that teaches people how to look and what is worthy of notice. Less willing to engage the educational force of the larger culture seriously as part of their political strategy, progressives have failed to theorize adequately how conservatives have seized upon this element of politics in ways that far outstrip its use by the left and other progressive forces. In other words, right-wing activities proceed more often than not unchallenged from a left that has never taken public pedagogy or the educational force of the larger culture seriously as part of its political strategy. In part, this use of the educational force of the culture explains both the rapid rise of the Tea Party movement and the fact that until recently it seems to have had no counterpart among progressives, especially young people, though this may change, given the arrogant and right-wing

---

4 See Gorski (2011). The study is taken from Arum and Roksa (2011).

attack being waged on unions, public sector workers, and public school educators in Wisconsin, Florida, Ohio, New Jersey, and other states where Tea Party candidates have come to power.[5]

In a social order dominated by the relentless privatizing and commodification of everyday life and the elimination of critical public spheres, young people find themselves in a society in which the formative cultures necessary for a democracy to exist have been more or less eliminated, reduced to spectacles of consumerism made palatable through a daily diet of game shows, reality TV, and celebrity culture. Yet, many young people are not producing their own news, cultures of resistance, and political modes of meaning through the new media, refusing altogether what the dominant media has to say. What many young people have come to recognize as particularly troubling is the absence in American society of vital formative cultures necessary to construct questioning agents who are capable of seeing through the consumer come-ons, and who can dissent and act collectively in an increasingly imperiled democracy. Instead of public spheres that promote dialogue, debate, and arguments with supporting evidence, American society offers young people a deeply depoliticized, conservative, de-formative culture through entertainment spheres that distort almost everything they touch. Celebrity culture has become a primetime fascination for many Americans and not only infantilizes any viable notion of agency but also legitimates opinions that utterly disregard evidence, reason, truth, and civility. Intimacy, long-term commitments, and the search for the good society are short-lived. The promise and pleasure of instant gratification cancel out the desire for freedom, reason, and responsibility.

Within the last 30 years, the United States under the reign of free-market fundamentalism has been transformed into a society that is more about forgetting than learning, more about consuming than producing, more about asserting private interests than democratic rights. As a long-term social investment, young people are now viewed as a liability, if not a pathology. No longer a symbol of hope and the future, they are viewed as a drain on the economy, and if they do not assume the role of functioning consumers, they are considered disposable. In a society obsessed with customer satisfaction and the rapid disposability of both consumer goods and long-term attachments, American youth are not encouraged to participate in politics. Nor are they offered the help, guidance, and modes of education that cultivate the capacities for critical thinking and engaged citizenship. Under such circumstances, thought cannot sustain itself and becomes short-lived, fickle, and ephemeral. If young people do not display a strong commitment to democratic politics and collective struggle, it is because they have lived

---

5 Surely, there is a certain irony in the fact that the work of Gene Sharp, a little-known American theorist in nonviolent action, is inspiring young people all over the world to resist authoritarian governments. Yet, his work is almost completely ignored by young people in the United States. See, for instance, Stolberg (2011: A1). See, in particular, Sharp (2012).

through 30 years of what I have elsewhere called "a debilitating and humiliating dis-investment in their future," especially if they are marginalized by class, ethnicity, and race.[6] What is new about this generation of young people is that they have experienced first-hand the relentless spread of a **neoliberal** pedagogical apparatus with its celebration of an unbridled individualism and its near-pathological disdain for community, public values, and the public good. They have been inundated by a market-driven value system that encourages a culture of competitiveness and produces a theater of cruelty. If American students have not until recently protested in large numbers the ongoing intense attack on higher education and the welfare state, it may be because they have been born into a society that is tantamount to what Alex Honneth describes as "an abyss of failed sociality [one in which] their perceived suffering has still not found resonance in the public space of articulation" (Honneth 2009: 188).

Of course, there are students in the United States who are involved in protesting the great injustices they see around them, including the wars in Afghanistan and Iraq, the corruption of American politics by casino capitalism, a permanent war economy, and the growing disinvestment in public and higher education. But, until the rise of the occupy movements, they have indeed been a minority, and not because they are part of what is often called a "failed generation." On the contrary, the failure lies elsewhere and points to the psychological and social consequences of growing up under a neoliberal regime that goes to great lengths to privatize hope, derail public values, and undercut political commitments. As the economic situation gets worse and the political stalemate continues under Republican Party rule, young people are now being forced to mobilize and resist the horrible conditions under which so many are living their lives. The Occupy Wall Street movement is a beginning, suggesting that more and more young people in cities all across the United States and Canada are now willing to create new social movements challenging the criminal behavior of Wall Street and the financial elite. What is truly remarkable about this movement is its emphasis on connecting learning to social change and its willingness to do so through new and collective modes of education. What is so encouraging in the Occupy Movement is that it views its very existence and collective identity as part of a larger struggle for the economic, political, and social conditions that give meaning and substance to what it means to make a radical democracy possible. One of the most famous slogans of May 1968 was "Be realistic, demand the impossible." The spirit of that slogan is alive once again. But what is different this time is that it appears to be more than a slogan, it now echoes throughout the United States and abroad as both a discourse of critique and a vocabulary of hope and long-term collective struggle. The current right-wing politics of illiteracy, exploitation, and cruelty can no longer hide in the cave of ignorance, legitimated by its shameful accomplices in the dominant media. The lights have come on in cities all over

---

6 Sharp (2012), p. 235. I have also taken up this theme in great detail in Giroux (2009b).

the United States and young people, workers, and other progressives are on the move. Thinking is no longer seen as an act of stupidity, acting collectively is no longer viewed as unimaginable, young people are no longer willing to be defined as disposable, and democracy is no longer accepted as an excess.

Young people need to be educated both as a condition of autonomy and for the sustainability of democratization as an ongoing movement. Not only does a substantive democracy demand citizens capable of self- and social criticism, but it also requires a critical formative culture in which people are provided with the knowledge and skills to be able to participate in such a society. What we see in the struggle for educational reforms in Europe and the Middle East is a larger struggle for the economic, political, and social conditions that give meaning and substance to what it means to make democracy possible. When we see 15-year-olds battle the established oppressive orders in the streets of Paris, Cairo, London, and Athens for a more just society, they offer a glimpse of the true potential of youth as a constructive force for trouble-making. But this expression of trouble exceeds the dominant society's eagerness to view youth as pathological, as monsters, and as a drain on the market-driven order. Instead, trouble in this sense speaks to something more suggestive of what John and Jean Comaroff call the "productive unsettling of dominant epistemic regimes under the heat of desire, frustration, or anger" (ibid.: 268). The expectations that frame market-driven societies are losing their grip on young people who can no longer be completely seduced or controlled by the tawdry promises and failed returns of corporate-dominated and authoritarian regimes.

These youth movements tell us that the social visions embedded in casino capitalism and deeply authoritarian regimes have lost both their utopian thrust and their ability to persuade and intimidate through threats, coercion, and state violence. Rejecting the terrors of the present and the modernist dreams of progress at any cost, young people have become, at least for the moment, harbingers of democracy fashioned through the desires, dreams, and hopes of a world based on the principles of equality, justice, and freedom. They point to a world order in which the future will certainly not mimic the present. What might be characterized by some commentators as an outburst of youthful utopianism reminiscent of the 1960s may in fact be the outcome of a pressing and very immediate reality. Youth culture has proven to be global in its use of new media, music, and fashion, and increasingly in terms of its collective anger against deep-seated injustice and its willingness to struggle against such forces. What we are witnessing at the current moment is American youth who recognize that they, too, are more than consumers; that market-driven society is not synonymous with democracy; that private rights are not more important than the social good; and that society's view of them as pathological and disposable demands a call for massive resistance in the streets, schools, and every other public space in which justice and democracy matter.

In pointing throughout this book to the ways in which free-market fundamentalism and the emerging culture of cruelty bear down on young people, I don't want to suggest that because neoliberal social formations appear to be winning in the United States that they have won or that the struggle is over. I think it is too easy to slide from an analysis of such dominant forces to erasing the important issue that this is a struggle that operates within a number of different contexts and is ongoing, however sporadic. As Lawrence Grossberg has pointed out,

> The fact that one can read for example a culture of cruelty off of various articulations does not yet mean that this is how young people live their lives. The fact that the cultural discourses are saturated with market logics does not mean that people live their lives with markets as the only definition/locus of value.
>
> (Personal Correspondence, June 18, 2011)

We have seen young people mobilize at the Seattle protests; they have mobilized against the war in Iraq and against tuition increases; and they have been part of intensive efforts at the global Social Forum to unite various modes of resistance; and they are now mobilizing in cities across America against corporate fraud, greed, and cruelty. As these new social formations and protests take place within and across diverse contexts, we need a new language for describing the nature of such forces, the complexity of such efforts, and the diverse terrains on which they operate. Youth do not at the current time inhabit what might be called an accomplished and sutured terrain of domination. In fact, youth in the present historical conjuncture increasingly locate themselves within complex and ongoing spheres of struggle that need to be deepened and expanded. Young people are coming alive with a passion for justice, dignity, and democracy in the United States and many other parts of the world. While there are no guarantees that they will prevail, a new sense of hope and possibility is in the air. Let us both organize and hope, struggle and move forward. This is a historical moment in which hope in the future seems likely—a moment in which the promise of democracy is as desirable as it is possible.

References

Alexander, Michelle. 2010. *The New Jim Crow: Mass Incarceration in the Age of Colorblindness*. New York: New Press.

Arum, Richard, and Josipa Roksa. 2011. *Academically Adrift: Limited Learning on College Campuses*. Chicago: University of Chicago Press.

Bacevich, Andrew. 2005. *The New American Militarism*. New York: Oxford University Press.

———. 2009. *Limits of Power*. New York: Holt Paperbacks.

———. 2010. *Washington Rules: America's Path to Permanent War*. New York: Metropolitan Books.

Balibar, Etienne. 2004. *We, The People of Europe? Reflections on Transnational Citizenship*. Princeton: Princeton University Press.

Bauman, Zygmunt. 2008. *The Art of Life*. London: Polity Press.

Bunch, Will. 2010. *The Backlash: Right-Wing Radicals, High-Def Hucksters and Paranoid Politics in the Age of Obama*. New York: Harper.

Butler, Judith. 2004. *Precarious Life: The Powers of Mourning and Violence*. London: Verso Press.

Child Trends. 2010. "Census Reports More Children Living in Poverty: Implications for Well-being." *Child Trends—Research Update* (September 16). Available online at http://archive.constantcontact.com/fs008/1101701160827/archive/1103693115054.html

Christine, C. 2010. "Kaiser Study: Kids 8 to 18 Spend More Than Seven Hours a Day With Media." *Spotlight on Digital Media and Learning: MacArthur Foundation* (January 21). Available online at http://spotlight.macfound.org/blog/entry/kaiser_study_kids_age_8_to_18_spend_more_than_seven_hours_a_day_with_media

Dionne, Jr., E. J. 2010. "The Tea Party: Tempest in a Very Small Teapot." *Washington Post* (September 23): A27.

Douglass, Frederick. 1985. "The Significance of Emancipation in the West Indies," speech given in Canandaigua, New York, August 3, 1857. P. 204 in *The Frederick Douglass Papers. Series One: Speeches, Debates, and Interviews. Volume 3: 1855–63*, ed. John W. Blassingame. New Haven: Yale University Press.

Dreier, Peter. 2007. "Bush's Class Warfare." *Huffington Post* (December 21). Available online at http://www.huffingtonpost.com/peter-dreier/bushs-class-warfare_b_77910.html

Durand, Jean-Marie. 2009. "For Youth: A Disciplinary Discourse Only," trans. Leslie Thatcher. *TruthOut.org* (November 15). Available online at http://www.truthout.org/11190911

Eckholm, Erik. 2010a. "Recession Raises Poverty Rate to a 15-Year High." *The New York Times* (September 16): A1.

———. 2010b. "School Suspensions Lead to Legal Challenge." *The New York Times* (March 18): A14.

Edelman Boren, Mark. 2001. *Student Resistance: A History of the Unruly Subject*. New York: Routledge.

Editorial. 2009. "The New Debtors' Prisons." *The New York Times* (April 5): A24.

Engelhardt, Tom. 2010. "An American World War: What to Watch for in 2010." *TruthOut.org* (January 3). Available online at http://www.truth-out.org/topstories/10410vh4

Everson, Carly. 2010. "Ind. Officer Uses Stun Gun on Unruly 10-Year-Old." *AP News* (April 1). Available online at http://www.guardian.co.uk/world/feedarticle/9014651

Felman, Shoshana, and Dori Laub. 1992. *Testimony: Crises of Witnessing in Literature, Psychoanalysis, and History*. New York: Routledge.

Francis, David R. 2006. "What A New 'Gilded Age' May Bring." *Christian Science Monitor* (March 6). Available online at http://www.csmonitor.com/2006/0306/p16s01-coop.html

Fuentes, Annette. 2011. *Lockdown High: When the Schoolhouse Becomes a Jailhouse*. New York: Verso.

Germano, Beth. 2010. "Worcester Teacher Accused of Abusing Autistic Boy." *The Autism News* (March 23). Available online at http://www.theautismnews.com/tag/abuse

Giroux, Henry A. 2001. *Stealing Innocence: Corporate Culture's War on Children*. New York: St. Martin's Press.

———. 2004. *The Abandoned Generation*. New York: Palgrave.

———. 2008. *Against the Terror of Neoliberalism*. Boulder, CO: Paradigm Publishers.

———. 2009a. "Schools and the Pedagogy of Punishment." *Truthout.org* (October 20). Available online at http://www.truth-out.org/10200910

———. 2009b. *Youth in a Suspect Society: Democracy or Disposability?* New York: Palgrave Macmillan.

Giroux, Henry A., and Susan Searls Giroux. 2004. *Take Back Higher Education: Race, Youth, and the Crisis of Democracy in the Post Civil Rights Era*. New York: Palgrave.

Goldstein, Amy. 2010. "Two Views about What Government Needs to Do about Poverty." *Washington Post* (September 16). Available online at http://www.washingtonpost.com/wp-dyn/content/article/2010/09/16/AR2010091606377.html

Gorski, Eric. 2011. "45% of Students Don't Learn Much In College." *Huffington Post* (January 21). Available online at http://www.huffingtonpost.com/2011/01/18/45-of-students-dont-learn_n_810224.html

Grossberg, Lawrence. 2001. "Why Does Neo-Liberalism Hate Kids? The War on Youth and the Culture of Politics." *The Review of Education/Pedagogy/Cultural Studies* 23(2): 111–36.

Hacker, Jacob S., and Paul Pierson. 2010. *Winner-Take-All Politics*. New York: Simon and Schuster.

Harvey, David. 2005. *A Brief History of Neoliberalism*. New York: Oxford University Press.

———. 2010. *The Enigma of Capital and the Crisis of Capitalism*. New York: Oxford University Press.

Head, Simon. 2011. "The Grim Threat to British Universities." *New York Review of Books* (January 13). Available online at http://www.nybooks.com/articles/archives/2011/jan/13/grim-threat-british-universities

Hedges, Chris. 2009. "The False Idol of Unfettered Capitalism." *Truthdig.com* (March 16). Available online at http://www.truthdig.com/report/item/20090316_the_false_idol_of_unfettered_capitalism

———. 2010. *Death of the Liberal Class*. Toronto: Knopf Canada.

Herbert, Bob. 2007. "Arrested While Grieving." *The New York Times* (May 26): A25.

———. 2009. "Stacking the Deck Against Kids." *The New York Times* (November 28): A19.

———. 2010. "Two Different Worlds." *The New York Times* (September 17): A31.

Hofstadter, Richard. 1964. "The Paranoid Style in American Politics." *Harper's* (November): 77–86.

Honneth, Alex. 2009. *Pathologies of Reason*. New York: Columbia University Press.

Johnson, Chalmers. 2006. *Nemesis: The Last Days of the American Empire*. New York: Metropolitan Books.

Judt, Tony. 2010. *Ill Fares the Land*. New York: Penguin.

Lewin, Tamar. 2010. "If Your Kids Are Awake, They're Probably Online." *The New York Times* (January 20): A1.

Liptak, Adam. 2007. "Lifers as Teenagers, Now Seeking a Second Chance." *The New York Times* (October 17): A1.

Martin, Courtney. 2010. *Do It Anyway: A New Generation of Activists*. Boston: Beacon Press.

Mascriotra, David. 2010. "The Rich Get Richer and the Young Go Into Deep Debt." *BuzzFlash* (December 6). Available online at http://blog.buzzflash.com/node/12045

Mayer, Jane. 2010. "Covert Operations: The Billionaire Brothers Who Are Waging a War Against Obama." *The New Yorker* (August 20). Available online at http://www.newyorker.com/reporting/2010/08/30/100830fa_fact_mayer

Morello, Carol. 2010. "About 44 Million in U.S. Lived below Poverty Line in 2009, Census Data Show." *Washington Post* (September 16). Available online at http://www.washingtonpost.com/wp-dyn/content/article/2010/09/16/AR2010091602698.html

Nancy, Jean-Luc. 2010. *The Truth of Democracy*, trans. Pascale-Anne Brault and Michael Naas. New York: Fordham University Press.

Pilger, John. 2011. "The Revolt in Egypt Is Coming Home." *Truthout.org* (February 10). Available online at http://www.truth-out.org/the-revolt-egypt-is-coming-home67624

Pitt, William Rivers. 2010. "Sick Bastards." *Truthout.org* (September 22). Available online at http://www.truth-out.org/sick-bastards63456

Price, Dick. 2011. "More Black Men Now in Prison System Than Were Enslaved." *LA Progressive* (March 31). Available online at http://www.zcommunications.org/more-black-men-now-in-prison-system-than-enslaved-in-1850-by-dick-price

Reich, Robert. 2010. "The Attack on American Education." *ReaderSupportedNews.org* (December 23). Available online at http://www.readersupportednews.org/opinion2/299-190/4366-the-attack-on-american-education

Robbins, Christopher. 2009. *Expelling Hope*. New York: SUNY Press.

Roberts, Dorothy. 2008. *Shattered Bonds: The Color of Child Welfare*. New York: Basic Civitas Books.

Schell, Jonathan. 2011. "Cruel America." *The Nation* (September 28). Available online at http://www.thenation.com/article/163690/cruel-america

Schwalbe, Michael. 2008. *Rigging the Game: How Inequality Is Reproduced in Everyday Life*. New York: Oxford University Press.

Searls Giroux, Susan. 2010. *Between Race and Reason: Violence, Intellectual Responsibility, and the University to Come*. Stanford: Stanford University Press.

Shakir, Faiz, Benjamin Armbruster, George Zornick, Zaid Jilani, Alex Seitz-Wald, and Tanya Somanader. 2010. "Intolerable Poverty in a Rich Nation." *The Progress Report* (September 20). Available online at http://pr.thinkprogress.org/2010/09/pr20100920/index.html

Sharp, Gene. 2012. *From Dictatorship to Democracy*. London: Serpent's Tail.

Simon, Jonathan. 2007. *Governing Through Crime: How the War on Crime Transformed American Democracy and Created a Culture of Fear*. New York: Oxford University Press.

Stolberg, Sheryl Gay. 2011. "Shy U.S. Intellectual Created Playbook Used in Revolution." *The New York Times* (February 16): A1.

Talley, Simeon. 2010. "Why Aren't Students in the U.S. Protesting Tuition, Too?" *Campus Progress* (December 23). Available online at http://www.campusprogress.org/articles/why_arent_students_in_the_u.s._protesting_tuition_too

Wacquant, Loïc. 2005. "Symbolic Power in the Rule of the 'State Nobility.'" Pp. 133–50 in *Pierre Bourdieu and Democratic Politics*, ed. Loïc Wacquant. London: Polity Press.

———. 2009. *Punishing the Poor: The Neoliberal Government of Social Insecurity*. Durham: Duke University Press.

Wa Thiong'o, Ngugi. 1993. *Moving the Centre: The Struggle for Cultural Freedom*. London: James Currey.

WFTV.com. 2007. "Kindergarten Girl Handcuffed, Arrested at Fla. School." (March 30). Available online at http://www.wftv.com/news/11455199/detail.html

Wilkinson, Richard, and Kate Pickett. 2010. *The Spirit Level: Why Equality Is Better for Everyone*. New York: Penguin Books.

Williams, Jeffrey. 2008. "Student Debt and the Spirit of Indenture." *Dissent* (Fall). Available online at http://www.dissentmagazine.org/article/?article=1303

Wolff, Richard D. 2010. "Austerity: Why and for Whom?" (July 4). Available online at http://www.rdwolff.com/content/austerity-why-and-whom

Wolin, Sheldon S. 2008. *Democracy Incorporated: Managed Democracy and the Specter of Inverted Totalitarianism*. Princeton, NJ: Princeton University Press.

Žižek, Slavoj. 2008. *Violence*. New York: Picador.

Glossary/Index

A

Alexander, Michelle 35

American political landscape: President Johnson's Great Society policies 16, 31–2; racial jibing 28–30; right-wing dominance xiv, xvii, 17–23, 34, 44–5; youth activism 39–48

Arendt, Hannah 18

Arizona shootings 34–5

Arum, Richard 43–4

authoritarianism: a form of rule whereby people are denied their democratic rights and a role in self-governance. The new authoritarianism under **neoliberalism** is based on a relationship between the state and the economy that produces rigid hierarchies, concentrates power in the hands of a financial and corporate elite, promotes a **culture of cruelty** based on a rabid individualism, transforms the welfare state into a punishing state, sacrifices civil liberties in the name of national security, labels any form of dissent as unpatriotic, and incarcerates large segments of populations deemed disposable 18–19, 33, 36–8

B

Balibar, Etienne 34

basketball 9–10, 11, 25–6, 27

Bauman, Zygmunt 19

Beck, Glenn 21, 29, 31

bin Laden, Osama, public response to his death 18

border crossing: the process of moving across or transgressing socially constructed barriers based on differences in race, gender, culture, ideology, and/or social position 10, 13–14, 26–7

Boston University 12, 13

Bourdieu, Pierre 28, 36

Bush, George H. W. election campaign 28–9

Butler, Judith 19

C

capitalism *see* **neoliberalism**

carceral state *see* **punishing/carceral state**

Carnegie-Mellon University 12

casino capitalism: a term describing how a handful of private interests seek to maximize their profits by manipulating the market to the detriment of social stability and the collective good. Proceeding outside of democratic accountability, corporations play games with market mechanisms that are poorly understood and risk negative social impacts (e.g., the subprime mortgage crisis in the United States) xiv–xv, xvii, 1–2, 37; see also **neoliberalism**

Cheney, Dick 18

children *see* youth/young people

citizenship xiii, xiv, 1, 35–6, 43, 45, 47

class 13, 24–8, 29, 31, 32, 39–40

collective responsibility *see* social responsibility

colleges xv, 3, 7, 12–13, 39–44, 46

Comaroff, Jean 47

Comaroff, John 47

commodification of youth: targeted as a market for commercial growth, young people are subjected to mass advertising campaigns that not only encourage youth to identify primarily as consumers and engage in a rampant consumer culture, but also objectify youth themselves as commodities for exploitation by market forces xiv, xvi, 4–5, 22, 45

community 15–16, 22, 24–5, 46

corporate sovereignty: the phenomenon by which corporations exhibit autonomous rule over their own affairs unrestricted by government regulation. Under such conditions, corporations increasingly exercise a mode of power over decisions of life and death once assumed by the state. As corporate power lays siege to the political process, the benefits flow to the rich and powerful. The term also suggests the concomitant weakening of traditional forms of nation-state sovereignty in the face of globalized corporate power 1, 2, 20–2

corporatization of higher education: as non-commodified public spheres come under the increasing influence of **neoliberalism**, the process whereby all aspects of higher education are subjected to the corporate drive for efficiency, downsizing, profit-making, and instrumentalist notions of excellence. The purpose of education is reduced to providing students with a set of skills and techniques so they can achieve employment, rather than educating them to be active, engaged and **critical citizens** xv, 7, 43, 44

crime-control complex *see* **youth crime-control complex**

criminalization: of social problems xvii, 2, 3, 35, 36; of youth *see* **youth crime-control complex**

critical citizenship: form of citizenship whereby individuals are self-conscious about politics, develop a sense of critical agency, embrace dialogue and self-reflection, question the nature of authority and are fully engaged in civic life with the purpose of governing and not simply being governed xiii, xiv, 1, 35–6, 43, 45, 46; *see also* **formative culture**

critical thinking/analysis 6, 42, 43–4, 45

cruelty, theater of *see* **culture of cruelty**

cultural apparatus: a concept developed by sociologist C. Wright Mills, referring to the material structures and social networks (e.g., the media) behind the dissemination of public pedagogy 3, 28, 30, 32, 36, 44; *see also* mass media

cultural capital: A term used by the sociologist Pierre Bourdieu to describe how an individual's possession of particular forms of learning and expression is vested with meaning and value by the broader culture. For example, consumer habits or "tastes" become signifiers of a person's class and social status, and thus forms of symbolic power 28; *see also* working class culture

cultural pedagogy *see* **public pedagogy**

culture: educational force *see* **formative culture**; prevailing culture of cruelty *see* **culture of cruelty**; working class culture 9–11, 13–14, 15–16, 24–6

culture of cruelty: a phenomenon characterized by a growing public fascination with violent media spectacles and competition, a survival-of-the-fittest mentality, and indifference—even contempt—toward the suffering of other human beings. Exemplified by the discourses of humiliation used by politicians and other public figures, the culture of cruelty legitimates and registers the powerful influence of neoliberal **public pedagogy** in fostering a disdain for anyone who does not believe the market is synonymous with justice and equality or who does not support individualized market solutions to social problems xv–xvi, 1, 5–6, 17–20, 34–7; *see also* criminalization; race/racism; social protections/safety net

D

democracy: crisis of xiii–xvii, 1–2, 8, 21–3, 32; reconstruction xvii–xviii, 4, 7–8, 32–3, 37–8, 39–48

democratic public spheres: institutional and cultural spaces in which people are presented with the time and opportunity to understand and influence the larger educational forces and politics that shape their lives. Such public spheres are crucial features of a civil society that supports the bonds of sociality and reciprocity in addition to individual self-determination. Educational and other public spheres are spaces of politics, power, and authority that require constant questioning in order to enable people to imagine changing the world around them so as to expand and deepen its democratic possibilities: access to xiv, xvii, 1, 41, 44, 45; construction/reclamation of 7, 8, 38, 46

DiMaeo, Leo 16

disposability: a set of ideas and practices characterized by a ruthless indifference to human suffering whereby the most brutalizing forces of capitalism are unleashed on individuals and communities who are increasingly denied the protections of the social state. Under such conditions certain groups such as immigrants, poor minority youth, and those individuals considered bad consumers are viewed as excess, waste, and expendable 18–22; academics 13; poor populations 3, 17, 19, 20, 21–2, 37; treatment of youth xv, 3, 5, 45, 47

Douglass, Frederick 8

Dreier, Peter 2

Dukakis, Michael 29

Durand, Jean-Marie 4

E

economic Darwinism: a concept that combines the values of unfettered self-interest with the notion of **free-market fundamentalism** whereby the economy becomes the central force determining who is fit to survive and who is considered disposable 2, 22, 42; *see* also **disposability**

Edelman Boren, Mark 40–1

education *see* **formative culture**; higher education; schools

Equal Justice Initiative report on life sentences for child criminals xvi

Expelling Hope (Robbins) 6

F

Felman, Shoshana 14

formative culture: the conditions that shape individuals within a given society. A critical formative culture includes the creation of **democratic public spheres** where individuals can be nurtured as political agents equipped with the skills, capacities, and knowledge they need to participate in the struggle for substantive and inclusive democracy. Today's formative culture in the United States is primarily commercial and disciplinary in nature, teaching people that self-expression is tied to acts of consumption, on the one hand, and that modes of competition, aggression, and control are necessary for survival, on the other 2, 37–8, 41, 45–6; *see also* **public pedagogy**

Freechild Project 38

free-market fundamentalism: the belief that a deregulated market should be the organizing principle for all political, social and economic decisions. Financial investments, market identities, atomizing social practices and commercial values take precedence over human needs, public responsibilities, and democratic relations xvii, 2; see also **casino capitalism**

fugitive/outlaw culture: a marginalized community or culture that is subordinate to the dominant culture. Such a culture may be seen as a threat to the dominant culture and its members suffer from the power, violence, and cruelty of dominant cultural institutions. While belonging to such a culture may be experienced as a deprivation or restriction when contrasted with the privilege afforded members of the dominant culture, it can also become a source of alternative knowledges, complex negotiations, resistance, solidarity, agency, and empowerment in relation to the dominant culture 10, 13–14

Johnson, President Lyndon 16, 31–2
Judt, Tony 2–3

K
Kaiser Family Foundation, study on youth use of electronic media 4
Katrina (hurricane) *see* Hurricane Katrina

L
Laub, Dori 14
Lewin, Tamar 4
Limbaugh, Rush 21, 29
Loughner, Jared Lee 34

M
Martin, Courtney 39–40
Mascriotra, David 43
mass media: treatment of youth xiv, xv, xvi, 4–5, 45; vehicle for **culture of cruelty**
    20, 28–31, 35–7
Media Education Foundation 38
medical care *see* health care
Medicare 7, 17
memory-work: the process of remembering through which a person reflects on his
    or her history, social position and the cultural forces that impacted his or her
    identity formation in order to imagine the possibilities for personal and social
    change 14, 27–8, 38
military spending 43
Mills, C. Wright 28
music, defining force in author's formative years 10, 14, 26, 28
muslims 30, 32

N
Nancy, Jean-Luc 43
neoliberalism: a system that emerged in the last 30 years whose primary goal is to
    promote a more expansive and brutal form of market capitalism through market
    derugulation, reduced corporate taxes, the shrinking of government intervention
    (i.e., the welfare state) and the privatization of public goods. Neoliberalism has
    increasing influence across the globe as it spreads its ideology through forms of
    public pedagogy that redefine citizenship as consumerism, celebrate a ruthless
    competitive individualism and seek to convince people of the unquestionable
    benefits of market forces. This neoliberal **cultural apparatus** in its varied forms
    cancels out or devalues gender, class-specific, and racial injustices of the existing

social order by absorbing the democratic impulses and practices of civil society within economic relations. Finally, **neoliberalism** produces, legitimates, and exacerbates the existence of persistent poverty, a narrowed conception of human rights, and growing inequalities between the rich and the poor 1–4, 7, 16–17, 32, 43, 45–8; *see also* **casino capitalism**; right-wing politics

new barbarians 17–18, 20, 21; *see also* right-wing politics

Ngugi Wa Thiong'o xiii

O

Obama, Barak 17, 18, 29, 30

Occupy Wall Street movement xviii, 42, 46

outlaw culture *see* **fugitive/outlaw culture**

P

Palin, Sarah 21, 29, 34

Pell Grants 42

Penna, Tony 12

performative nature of race and class: the idea that forms of individual self-expression (gestures, speech, and actions) work in tandem with the perceptions of others to constitute a person's belonging to a particular community based on a common racial or class identity 24–8

Perry, Rick 29

Pilger, John 39

political landscape of America *see* American political landscape

politics of humiliation *see* **culture of cruelty**

poverty/poor populations: disposability 3, 17, 19, 20, 21–2, 37; education cuts affecting 42; welfare reform for 7, 32

prisons xvi, 2, 3, 7, 21, 32; *see also* **punishing/carceral state**

privatization 1, 2, 44

public good: higher education 39, 40, 43, 44; *see also* social responsibility; welfare system/public services

public pedagogy: a powerful ensemble of ideological and institutional forces whose aim is to use the educational force of the larger culture to produce, disseminate, and circulate ideas. Corporate-driven public pedagogy and culture aim to produce competitive, self-interested individuals vying for their own material and ideological gain. As such, under **neoliberalism**, public pedagogy has become a reactionary force as it operates from a variety of educational sites through forms of pedagogical address in which personal agency, social solidarity, and the obligations of citizenship necessary for a functioning democracy are reduced to a burden or unfortunate constraint. Matters of formerly public concern are reconfigured as utterly private miseries, and individuals are blamed for their living conditions rather than seen as entitled to social support xvi, xvii–xviii, 4–5, 36–7, 38, 44; new racist cultural pedagogy 28–31

public services/welfare system: importance to democracy 7, 32; under **neoliberalism** iv, 1–2, 17, 18, 21, 35

public spheres/spaces 9, 17; *see also* **democratic public spheres**

punishing/carceral state: increasingly related to the hollowing out of the social state, which gives way to the rise of the punishing, it refers generally to a state reconfigured into a carceral enterprise more concerned with punishing and policing than with nurturing and investing in the public good. Working in conjunction with a growing emphasis on security and surveillance, an expanding prison-industrial complex, and a culture of fear promoted by the mass media, U.S. state governments now invest more in prison construction than in education xv–xvi, 2, 3, 5–6, 19, 35–7

R

race/racism xv, 10, 24–32

Reagan, Ronald 1, 40

Reich, Robert 42

reverse racism 29

right-wing politics xiv, xvii, 17–23, 34, 44–5; on campus 40, 42, 44; racist cultural pedagogy 28–30

Robbins, Christopher 6

Roberts, Dorothy 7

Roksa, Josipa 43–4

S

Schell, Jonathan 18, 34

Schlessinger, Laura 29

schools 22; discipline/punishment xv–xvi, 3, 5–6, 7, 16, 36; performative categories in (race/class) 24–7, 32, 35

school-to-prison pipeline 7; *see also* **youth crime-control complex**

Searls Giroux, Susan 40

Silber, John 12

Smith Hill neighbourhood, Providence, Rhode Island 9–10, 11, 15, 16, 24–7

social contract xiii–xiv, xvi, 3, 15, 22, 45

social protections/safety net: democratic significance 7, 32; neoliberalist attack on iv, 1–2, 17–18, 19, 21, 35

social responsibility (idea of): collective struggle to reassert 38, 39, 41, 47; lost in a market-driven society 1, 2, 15, 19, 37, 46; presence in 1950s/60s working class neighbourhoods 14, 15–16, 22; replacement by individualism/instant gratification 19–20, 21–2, 35–6, 45; youth as a marker for xiii, xiv, xvi–xvii, 4, 22; *see also* public good

"soft war" (against youth) *see* **commodification of youth**

state torture 18, 36

student demonstrations 39–44

stun guns, use on children 6

T

Talley, Simeon 40

Tea Party 20, 21, 44–5

testimony *see* **witnessing/testimony**

theater of cruelty *see* **culture of cruelty**

Tuttle, Steve (Taser International Inc.) 6

U

United Nations resolution on imprisonment of children xvi

universities *see* higher education

V

violence: by children 6, 9, 10, 13, 27; product of **culture of cruelty** 30, 31, 32, 34–5, 36, 37; youth rejection of 47

W

Wacquant, Loïc 3, 36

Walker, Scott 42

Wall Street, target for collective action xviii, 42, 46

wars: high expenditure 43; source of student protest 46, 48

Watson, Desre xvi, 6

wealth 21; rich/poor divide 2, 3–4, 17–18, 25; *see also* poverty/poor populations

welfare system/public services: reform 7, 32; under neoliberalism iv, 1–2, 17–18, 19, 21, 35

"Why Class Matters in Campus Activism?" (Martin) 39–40

Williams, Jeffrey 42–3

witnessing/testimony: an ethical response that involves telling one's story and listening to the stories of others as part of a broader social responsibility to engage the present. It involves both understanding the complex conditions, cultures and institutions that have shaped our individual and collective histories and connecting personal experiences to social issues as a means of fostering self-awareness and social transformation 14; author's testimony *see* Giroux, Henry A.

work, youth opportunities xvii, 3, 5, 7, 10, 11, 35

working class culture 9–11, 13–14, 15–16, 24–6

Y

youth crime-control complex: the cultural and structural elements that subject young people to disciplinary mechanisms within the broader society, including their criminalization and involvement with an expanding youth criminal justice system. The growing presence of police and security personnel in public schools means that schools become containment centers for populations of disposable youth, especially those marginalized by race and class, who are portrayed as dangerous and hardened criminals destined for incarceration. In contrast to other youth who are lured into a culture of consumerism, these youth face discipline for minor infractions and are ushered into a **school-to-prison pipeline** that offers little opportunity for escape. Youth facing social problems such as pervasive racism and poverty are thus often seen as "problem youth" rather than as youth with problems xv–xvi, 3, 4, 5–6, 16, 36

Z